The Declining Work
and Welfare of People
with Disabilities

The Declining Work and Welfare of People with Disabilities

What Went Wrong and a Strategy for Change

Richard V. Burkhauser and Mary C. Daly

The AEI Press

Publisher for the American Enterprise Institute

WASHINGTON, D.C.

Distributed by arrangement with the Rowman & Littlefield Publishing Group, 4501 Forbes Boulevard, Suite 200, Lanham, Maryland 20706. To order, call toll free 1-800-462-6420 or 1-717-794-3800. For all other inquiries, please contact AEI Press, 1150 Seventeenth Street, N.W., Washington, D.C. 20036, or call 1-800-862-5801.

Library of Congress Cataloging-in-Publication Data

Burkhauser, Richard V.
The declining work and welfare of people with disabilities: what went wrong and a strategy for change / Richard V. Burkhauser and Mary C. Daly.
    p. cm.
Includes bibliographical references and index.
ISBN-13: 978-0-8447-7215-8 (cloth)
ISBN-10: 0-8447-7215-1 (cloth)
ISBN-13: 978-0-8447-7217-2 (ebook)
ISBN-10: 0-8447-7217-8 (ebook)
    1. People with disabilitis—Employment—United States. 2. People with disabilities—Government policy—United States 3. People with disabilities—Government policy—Netherlands 4. Disability Insurance—Government policy—United States 5. Disability Insurance—Government policy—Netherlands. I. Daly, Mary C. (Mary Colleen) II. Title.
    HD7256.U5B868 2011
    362.4'045610973—dc23
                                                          2011021368

Printed in the United States of America

Contents

Acknowledgments

This book is based on over three decades of research by the authors, either jointly or with others—most especially Philip de Jong and Leo Aarts—in the growing area of the economics of disability. We thank our research colleagues and others, particularly Monroe Berkowitz and John Burton Jr., who have contributed to this developing literature. We especially thank our three anonymous referees for their careful reading of the first complete draft of this manuscript. We are grateful to Bruce Meyer and other participants at the 11th Annual Joint Conference of the Retirement Research Consortium, as well as John Bound, Nicole Maestas, Dave Stapleton, and other participants at the 2010 and 2011 Spring Meetings of the Michigan Retirement Research Center for their comments on later versions of the manuscript. We also are indebted to Andrew Houtenville, Katherine Thornton, Robert Weathers, and David Wittenburg for providing data for the book. We thank Jeff Larrimore and especially Joyce Kwok for exceptional research assistance and are grateful to Anita Todd for editorial assistance.

Finally, Richard V. Burkhauser thanks Henry Olsen for being a true sounding board for his early ideas on the book and providing him with an office at the American Enterprise Institute during the first semester of his sabbatical. Burkhauser also thanks Mark Wooden for providing him with an office in the Melbourne Institute of Applied Economic and Social Research at the University of Melbourne and leaving him alone to write during the second semester of his sabbatical.

List of Illustrations

TABLES

Introduction

United States disability program expenditures are rising at an unsustainable pace. Real costs for the disability insurance program—Social Security Disability Insurance (SSDI)—have increased substantially over time, with especially rapid growth over the last decade (see figure I-1). Both the Social Security Trustees and the Congressional Budget Office project that the system will be insolvent before the end of the decade.[1] Real costs for the means-tested disability program—Supplemental Security Income (SSI)— also have risen, and growth in both the disabled adults and disabled children components of the program has accelerated over time.

Table I-1 identifies what is driving these costs: an increasing fraction of those with work-limiting disabilities are out of the labor market and on federal disability benefits. In 1981, the first year the March Current Population Survey (CPS) collected such data, 7.3 percent of the working-age population (ages twenty-five to fifty-nine) reported having a health condition that affected their ability to work. Of this group, roughly 35 percent reported working in the previous year. Slightly fewer, 32.6 percent, reported receiving either SSDI or SSI benefits. In 2010, the most recent available year of CPS data, the percentage of the working-age population with a work-limiting disability was almost the same—7.8 percent—but the percentage employed—22.6 percent—and the percentage receiving SSDI or SSI benefits—51.4 percent—had changed substantially.[2]

In this book, we examine whether declining employment rates and rising disability rolls are inevitable consequences of worsening health or an aging population. Reviewing the research literature on the nature of disability, the evolution of health status, and the role of incentives in individual decisions, we conclude that this is not the case. Instead, we argue that these outcomes are consequences of changes in SSDI and SSI-disabled adults and

1

FIGURE I-1

SSDI, SSI-DISABLED ADULTS, AND SSI-DISABLED CHILDREN
PROGRAM COSTS OVER TIME

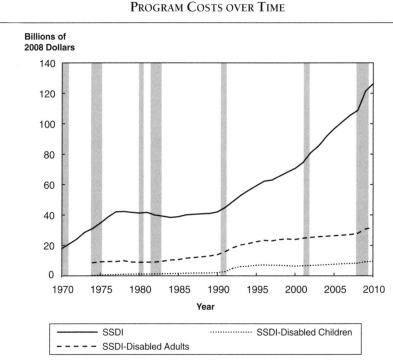

SOURCE: Social Security Administration 2009a, 2010a.
NOTE: Gray bars denote National Bureau of Economic Reseach (NBER) recessions.

TABLE I-1

EMPLOYMENT AND SSDI/SSA RECEIPT AMONG
POPULATION REPORTING WORK LIMITATION

Year	Work Limitation Prevalence	Employed More Than 200 Hours Last Year	SSDI/SSI Receipt
1981	7.3%	35.2%	32.6%
2010	7.8%	22.6%	51.4%

SOURCE: Authors' calculations using March Current Population Survey data.
NOTE: Sample limited to civilian noninstitutional population ages 25–59.

SSI-disabled children program rules and how program gatekeepers administer these rules.

Since past policy changes are the cause, future policy changes can be the solution. Drawing on lessons from two recent policy initiatives—the reform of U.S. welfare policy and the reform of Dutch disability policy—and using evidence of how program incentives affect behavior, we suggest fundamental changes in the way disability is insured and managed in the United States.

To understand and consider the proposals we offer, it is important to keep in mind the data in table I-1, which show that the population with disabilities is heterogeneous and that many of its members can and do work. Although the Social Security Administration (SSA), for the purpose of receiving SSDI or SSI benefits, requires applicants to demonstrate an inability to perform substantial gainful activity, researchers and advocates have long realized that such inabilities can have as much to do with social, cultural, and physical barriers as with the capacities of people with disabilities. This recognition culminated in the Americans with Disabilities Act of 1990 (ADA), which mandates, among other things, that people with disabilities are provided access to and accommodation in employment.

Unfortunately, while the ADA removed barriers to work, changes in the federal disability transfer programs—including SSDI, SSI-disabled adults, and SSI-disabled children—have made work less attractive and less profitable. Consequently, the share of adults with disabilities on either SSDI or SSI has continued to grow, as has the share of poor children with disabilities on SSI-disabled children benefits.[3]

These changes in the program incentives and the growth in the disability transfer rolls they have produced are undesirable for a number of reasons. First, by predicating disability benefits and support on demonstrating an inability to work, the system encourages individuals with health-based impairments to invest in not working in order to qualify for benefits. As we will show, this choice imposes real economic consequences on decision makers, since average benefits are lower than average wages and reentering the labor market after the absence required to receive benefits is generally difficult.[4] Second, by expanding disability cash-transfer programs while other nonwork transfer programs (such as welfare) were declining, the system unintentionally increased the relative value of moving onto the disability rolls, even for those who might otherwise choose to work. This has, in turn, increased the administrative burdens associated with determining which applicants qualify for benefits and which do not, ultimately boosting costs for taxpayers relative to other program designs. Finally, abstracting from the individual and social costs of the programs, the focus on cash assistance in lieu of earnings ignores the value of work itself. Work links individuals to the economy and to the returns of economic growth. Work also connects individuals socially and culturally, which is a goal of advocates for those with disabilities. Importantly, work is also a social expectation; this means exceptions to working generally come with a cost and are not granted lightly or without ongoing cause. The value of work—both to individuals and to the society that depends on everyone's productive effort—suggests that work, rather than benefits, should be the primary means for assisting and insuring those subject to disabilities and other negative economic shocks.

We begin the book by reviewing the context of our current situation. We show how patterns in disability program growth have been affected by policy changes that made access to disability benefits, conditioned on limited or no work, easier to obtain. We suggest that these changes encouraged workers with disabilities and the families of children with disabilities to move onto federally funded long-term disability transfer programs. Moreover, they encouraged employers and state governments to assist individuals with disabilities in obtaining federally provided benefits rather than investing in work and work-related activities. We argue that these policy changes and the incentives they created for individuals, employers, and states have driven the rapid decline in employment and the rise in disability-benefit receipt among the working-age population with disabilities documented in table I-1.

Two recent reformations of long-standing government programs—U.S. welfare and Dutch disability policy—offer support for the view that policy can affect outcomes and provide guidance for how changes to U.S. disability policy might proceed. A key lesson from the 1996 federal welfare reforms is that prowork incentives can increase employment and improve household incomes for vulnerable populations such as low-income single mothers. While welfare reform was not a panacea, the fact that large numbers of low-skilled single mothers, with support, could move into the labor market and reduce their dependence on federal welfare suggests that some number of adults with disabilities and nondisabled low-income parents of disabled children could also make this shift. Additional lessons come from recent disability reforms in the Netherlands, which curbed costs in the Dutch disability insurance system and reduced the size of the disability transfer population without increasing other social welfare-program rolls. The Dutch reforms suggest that prowork strategies can increase the employment rates of those with disabilities and decrease the disability insurance beneficiary population without leaving those who experience a health shock unprotected. Both reformations and the outcomes they produced highlight the power of incentives on the behavior of individuals targeted by government programs.

Although change is clearly possible, it is never easy. The 1996 welfare reforms occurred only after a consensus formed around the idea that the long-standing program was failing everyone, costing more for taxpayers while delivering fewer opportunities to single mothers. The same consensus of understanding led to the disability reforms in the Netherlands. Prior to its reform, the Dutch disability system was considered the worst in the industrialized world with respect to both its expenditure growth and its inability to keep people with disabilities in the labor market. In both the U.S. welfare and the Dutch disability cases, rapid growth in program rolls and expenses, coupled with long-run negative outcomes for the targeted population, produced a willingness to consider large-scale and fundamental changes to restructure the programs. The fundamental change that defined reforms in both programs was the shift in focus toward work. In the case of U.S. single mothers, this meant providing individuals with the incentives to work and state governments with the funds to make work profitable. In the case of the Dutch disability system, this meant providing workers and their employers with incentives to focus on a return to work following the onset of a disability. The lesson from both of these policy reforms is that coordinated efforts to encourage work and make work pay can have significant effects on the composition of income going to vulnerable groups and can slow the growth in publicly provided cash-benefit programs.

Book Overview

Chapter 1 reports the growth in SSDI and SSI caseloads and examines how the increased use of these programs has affected the income of working-age people with disabilities over the past thirty years. The data show that despite large increases in the prevalence of government benefits among Americans with disabilities, their household incomes have stagnated. This pattern contrasts sharply with that of single mothers, who experienced sizable reductions in benefits after welfare reform but saw their household incomes increase.

To learn from the relative economic progress single mothers made following welfare reform, chapter 2 explores the changes in public policies targeted toward them and examines how these changes altered the incentives for both individuals and states to invest in work over benefit receipt. The chapter concludes with a brief summary of how welfare reform affected single mothers.

In chapter 3, we return to the main focus of the book—the population with disabilities. We begin by describing what we mean by disability and how trends in health and functional limitations, which have not discernibly worsened, are at odds with data on disability benefit caseloads, which have grown over the past thirty years and rapidly since 1990. The rest of the chapter shows how changes in disability eligibility rules and changes in the interpretation and implementation of those rules have affected these trends. Of the three forces driving the growth in disability expenditures—demographic changes, economic conditions, and program changes—we argue that program changes have had the greatest effect. The key message in this chapter is that a health condition, impairment, or disability does not in itself define an individual's ability to work or determine the rise and fall of disability caseloads in the United States.

Accepting that health, inability to work, and disability caseloads are not completely correlated, in chapter 4 we show how the design of U.S. disability policy influences the likelihood that individuals who experience a health condition will apply for benefits over pursuing employment. We argue that a number of incentives have led to the following outcome as observed in the data: the population with disabilities has become increasingly reliant on cash transfers over earnings and is falling further and further behind the rest of the population.

In light of the U.S. experience, chapter 5 reviews the experience of the Netherlands, once thought to have the most excessive disability system in the industrialized world. In the 1980s, for every Dutch worker, one person was receiving disability benefits, three times the U.S. rate. After several failed attempts to modify the system, in 2002, the Dutch undertook more fundamental reform, initiating a series of measures intended to encourage work over benefit receipt. As a result, by 2009, the ratio of disability beneficiaries to workers in the Netherlands had dropped considerably, falling below that of the United States. The Dutch experience suggests that fundamental changes in longstanding disability programs are possible and can lead to positive outcomes.

In chapter 6, we shift our focus from the adult population with disabilities to the SSI-disabled children program. We show that this program also has expanded over time and is the subject of considerable concern. In part, this concern owes to program costs. More troubling, though, is the failure of SSI to integrate children with disabilities into the work-force when they become adults. We review the provisions and rules in the SSI-disabled children program and show how, as in the adult programs, the incentives embedded in the program make it vulnerable to growth unrelated to any real changes in children's health.

Building on lessons from U.S. welfare reform and Dutch disability reform, chapter 7 outlines the themes for fundamental structural reform to the U.S. disability system. As this book shows, the population with disabilities is heterogeneous and no single program will be able to meet all needs. As such, our primary recommendation is that policymakers adopt a work-first strategy for people with disabilities and pull forward the invest-ments in work currently targeted only on those already on the rolls. Doing so will eliminate the need for the counterintuitive policy currently in place in which the SSA provides access to work-focused support only after individuals have gone through an extended process of showing they are unable to work. We argue that encouraging work rather than benefit receipt following the onset of a disability will slow the process that eventually leads to an inability to work and can solve a range of problems currently burdening the disability system. Work-first strategies are consistent with the goals of the ADA, which call for the integration of people with disabilities into the labor market. They also provide a long-term opportunity for people with disabilities to reap some of the rewards of a growing economy, an opportunity not granted by the current cash-benefit system. Moreover, work-oriented approaches that make the returns to employment higher than the returns to benefit receipt assist program administrators in determining who is unable to work, thus limiting growth in the rolls caused by changes in enforcement or measurement issues. Finally, work-first strategies promote a fundamental change in the structure of support for people with disabilities that allows them access to the full social safety net provided to working-age adults.

Although work-first strategies are simple to talk about, they are difficult to implement. This difficulty is reflected in our proposals for SSDI and SSI, which are only sketches of possible paths to change. SSDI and SSI serve different populations, so we propose separate strategies for their reform.

For SSDI, we borrow from the lessons in the Netherlands to propose making cash benefits a last resort and available only after all attempts at accommodation and rehabilitation by both private- and public-sector service providers have failed. This orientation will improve outcomes on a number of fronts, including providing incentives for employers, employees, and private insurers to make continued employment a priority. Currently, the long-term SSDI transfer program does not coordinate federal and state government programs to provide short-term transfers or rehabilitation to workers who experience the onset of a disability. More importantly, there is no coordination between the private-sector provision of accommodation, rehabilitation, and short- and long-term transfer payments to these workers at the onset of a disability and the SSDI program that ultimately bears responsibility for providing long-term transfer payments to those who do not return to work. Because SSDI contributions are not experience rated, firms do not bear the full cost of decisions not to accommodate and rehabilitate employees to prevent their movement onto the SSDI rolls. Rewarding firms that reduce the likelihood that these workers will move onto the SSDI rolls by reducing their SSDI taxes and requiring firms that do not do this to pay higher SSDI taxes is a positive-sum game that can lower the costs of SSDI and increase employment for people with disabilities.

The proposals for SSI build on the idea that SSI is principally a welfare program targeted at low-income households whose members frequently have limited labor-market skills or work histories that exacerbate any health shocks that they experience. As such, we argue that SSI should be placed under state administration and control and integrated with other low-income support programs funded by Federal Temporary Assistance for Needy Families (TANF). The same holds for the SSI-disabled children program. Devolving the program to states would allow SSI to benefit from the experience gained from integrating low-income single mothers into the labor force. Moreover, we suggest that this devolution to states would enable the program more directly to provide disabled children with the specific educational and rehabilitative support they require to progress through school with the expectation that, like all other children, they will enter the labor force as adults.

The message of this book is straightforward: the U.S. disability system needs systemic reform. Our analysis suggests that such reform would be widely beneficial; done well, it would lower projected long-term costs for taxpayers, make the job of disability administrators less difficult, and, importantly, improve the short- and long-term opportunities for people with disabilities.

Note to Readers

To ensure that this book is accessible to a broad audience, we have attempted to keep the exposition free from technical details, including discipline-specific language, lengthy definitions, and discussions of methodology and data analysis. These details are available in the notes to the exhibits and in the data appendix at the end of the book.

1

The Economic Status of
People with Disabilities

Public policies aimed at protecting working-age men and women with disabilities generally focus on providing benefits in lieu of work. Social Security Disability Insurance and Supplemental Security Income both offer cash benefits to people with disabilities deemed unable to work.[1] SSDI is a social insurance program that provides cash transfers to working-age men and women based on their past labor earnings. Individuals who have contributed to the Social Security system sufficiently to be covered by SSDI and who demonstrate that they are unable to perform any substantial gainful activity because of a medical or functional limitation can receive benefits.[2] SSI includes two programs for disability: one for adults and one for children. The SSI-disabled adults program is a categorical, means-tested welfare program that provides cash transfers to adults who meet the same substantial gainful activity test as SSDI recipients but whose total family income and assets are below a certain maximum. The SSI-disabled children program, like the SSI-disabled adults program, is also a categorical, means-tested welfare program. It provides cash transfers to low-income families of children who meet the child version of the SSDI substantial gainful activity test. In addition to receiving cash transfers, recipients of SSDI and SSI benefits are eligible for health benefits under Medicare or Medicaid. Medicare is available after a two-year waiting period to those on SSDI. Medicaid is available immediately to SSI beneficiaries.

In the late 1980s and 1990s, the rules governing access to the SSDI and SSI-disabled adult and children programs were loosened and the incentives to enter the programs increased. Over the same period, access to cash benefits for another target of public policy—low-income single mothers—

declined as reforms leading up to and included in the Personal Responsibility and Work Opportunity Reconciliation Act of 1996 replaced the cash-based Aid to Families with Disabled Children (AFDC) with the work-based Temporary Assistance for Needy Families.[3] The outcomes of these different approaches to assisting people with disabilities and single mothers can be seen in figures 1-1 and 1-2.

FIGURE 1-1

PERCENTAGE OF POPULATION ON SSDI, SSI-DISABLED ADULTS,
AND SSI-DISABLED CHILDREN BENEFIT ROLLS OVER TIME

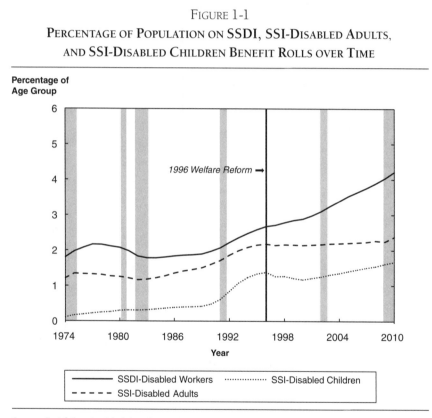

SOURCE: Social Security Administration, various years a.
NOTE: Gray bars denote NBER recessions.

Looking first at disability, figure 1-1 shows the increase over time in caseloads for SSDI and SSI-disabled adults and the SSI-disabled children programs as a share of the population in the respective age groups. As the figure shows, disability caseloads as a share of the population have risen

FIGURE 1-2

PERCENTAGE OF FAMILIES ON AFDC/TANF BENEFIT ROLLS OVER TIME

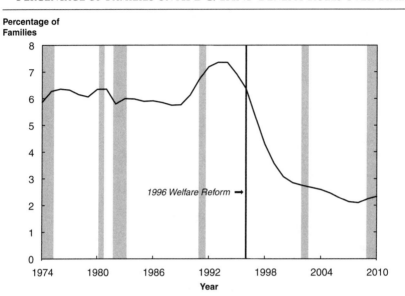

SOURCE: U.S. Department of Health and Human Services, various years.
NOTE: Gray bars denote NBER recessions.

substantially since the 1970s. SSDI caseloads grew dramatically in the 1970s, fell slightly in the early 1980s, and rose modestly from 1984 to 1989. Since 1990, however, caseload growth has been consistently rapid. Data on SSDI applications (not shown) point to more rapid future growth, as those who applied for benefits in the wake of the 2007–2008 recession move through the system and become part of the SSDI caseload. The SSI-disabled adults program has also grown substantially since its start in 1974; the greatest growth occurred over 1984–1996. Since 1996, caseloads have increased only slightly. However, as with SSI, growth in caseloads accelerated in 2010. The SSI-disabled children program grew little until the 1990 Supreme Court decision in the case of *Sullivan v. Zebley* required that the broader eligibility criteria for SSI-disabled adults also be used to determine eligibility in the SSI-disabled children program.[4] This led to rapid program growth until 1996 when, as part of welfare reform, the eligibility criteria for SSI-disabled children was decoupled from the one used for SSI-disabled adults and tightened.[5] In 2000, caseloads began to increase again and have risen steadily since.

A very different picture can be seen for AFDC/TANF caseloads. Figure 1-2 plots AFDC/TANF caseloads over time as a share of families. Following modest growth from 1974 through 1989, AFDC caseloads shot up, peaking in 1994. Following program changes leading up to and culminating in welfare reform, caseloads fell precipitously.[6] The largest decline in caseloads occurred from 1996 to 2000, a period of rapid economic expansion in the United States. Since 2000, caseloads have continued to fall, albeit much more gradually. In 2009 and 2010, caseloads ticked up somewhat in response to the severe economic disruptions caused by the recession. Given the magnitude of the recession, the uptick in TANF recipients is understandable.

As the figures highlight, the differences in policy treatments directed at people with disabilities and those directed at low-income single mothers have corresponded with significant divergences in their respective dependence on government cash transfers. This different treatment also has produced divergent economic outcomes. As the next section details, over the last two decades the median household income of working-age men and women with disabilities has remained flat and their labor earnings and employment have declined. In contrast, single mothers' household income, labor earnings, and employment have all risen, with especially large increases following the 1996 welfare reforms.

Relative Economic Status of People with Disabilities

There are many ways to compare the economic progress of different groups. We use a method common to the research and policy literature and contrast changes in median size-adjusted household income using data from the Current Population Survey (U.S. Department of Commerce, various years).[7] Figure 1-3 plots trends in this measure of income for men and women with disabilities, single mothers, and, for comparison, the entire working-age population. As the figure shows, median income for all working-age persons fluctuates with the business cycle; it rises during expansions and falls during recessions. The last few values in the series show the initial negative effects of the very severe recession that began in 2007.

FIGURE 1-3
SIZE-ADJUSTED HOUSEHOLD INCOME FOR
MEDIAN WORKING-AGE PERSONS OVER TIME

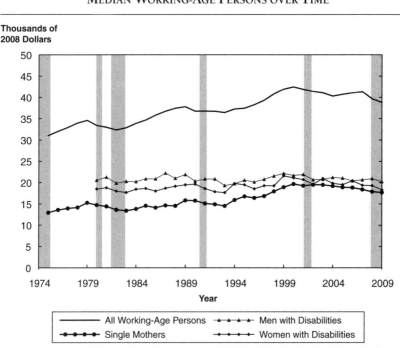

SOURCE: Authors' calculations using March CPS data.
NOTE: Gray bars denote NBER recessions.

With the sluggish pace of recovery, it is likely median household size–adjusted income will continue to drop beyond the data we show.

Not surprisingly, at any point in time, the median incomes for men and women with disabilities and single mothers are lower than the median income of the general population of working-age persons. Although these absolute differences are important, our focus here is on the extent to which these gaps have increased or decreased over time.

To do this analysis, we compare income changes between 1982, 1993, 2004, and 2009, years that correspond to the low points of median income following each of the recessions.[8] Here the data show little progress for people with disabilities. Although the median income of men and women with disabilities has varied over time, on net, both groups are relatively worse off than they were three decades ago. This is true whether people with disabilities are compared to all working age people or single mothers.

Given the aforementioned differences in federal cash support going to people with disabilities and low-income single mothers, the differential growth paths for their respective household incomes requires further examination. Table 1-1 compares the prevalence of five different sources of income in the households of all working-age persons with working-age men with disabilities, women with disabilities, and single mothers. In 1982, approximately 43 percent of men with disabilities had some labor earnings. This turns out to be the peak over the period examined; by 1993, only 39 percent had earnings, by 2004 only 29 percent had earnings, and in 2009 the number had fallen to 26 percent. As the percentage of men with disabilities with earnings fell, the percentage of men with either SSI/SSDI payments or public-assistance payments rose. In 1982, nearly one-third of working-age men with disabilities received SSI or SSDI; by 2009, just over half received one or the other of these benefits. The story for working-age women with disabilities is similar to that of working-age men with disabilities: the likelihood that these women would provide some labor earnings to their households declined over the entire period, from 31 percent in 1982 to 27.4 percent in 2004 to 23.4 percent in 2009. As for men with disabilities, as earnings rates fell for these women, rates of disability benefit receipt rose. By 2009, just over half of working-age women with disabilities received either SSI or SSDI benefits.

The trends were exactly reversed for single mothers. In 1982, 69 percent of single mothers provided some labor income to their households. This rose to 71 percent in 1993 and increased to more than 80 percent in 2004, near the percentage for all working-age households. The 2007–2009 recession reduced this contribution to just over 77 percent, a slightly larger reduction than observed for the entire working-age population. In 1982, 49.8 percent of single-mother households received some public-assistance income (from SSI/SSDI and other public assistance). This declined slightly in 1993 and dropped to 23.6 percent in 2004. In 2009, this number rose only slightly, to 26.1 percent.

Another way to understand the role of earnings and benefits in generating household income is to consider the importance of income

TABLE 1-1

PREVALENCE OF HOUSEHOLD INCOME BY SOURCE FOR
VULNERABLE WORKING-AGE PERSONS, SELECTED YEARS

		Own Labor Income	Others' Labor Income	Own SSI/SSDI	Own Public Assistance	All Other Income
	1982	78.8%	72.6%	3.6%	14.2%	78.2%
All Working-	1993	82.7%	73.1%	4.7%	11.6%	79.0%
Age Persons	2004	81.8%	70.6%	5.4%	6.3%	69.7%
	2009	80.1%	70.2%	5.6%	9.6%	67.1%
	1982	43.2%	57.2%	33.7%	32.6%	76.1%
Men with	1993	38.5%	55.5%	41.2%	25.7%	76.9%
Disabilities	2004	29.4%	51.4%	50.7%	17.7%	69.4%
	2009	26.1%	51.8%	51.4%	17.7%	68.6%
	1982	31.0%	61.2%	29.7%	20.3%	75.8%
Women with	1993	35.3%	55.7%	38.1%	22.5%	72.3%
Disabilities	2004	27.4%	51.2%	48.7%	14.0%	69.2%
	2009	23.4%	50.2%	51.7%	12.0%	66.9%
	1982	68.8%	35.4%	11.4%	38.4%	63.4%
Single	1993	71.1%	35.3%	12.1%	36.0%	66.9%
Mothers	2004	80.1%	36.3%	9.5%	14.1%	64.9%
	2009	77.3%	37.5%	10.1%	15.8%	63.1%

SOURCE: Authors' calculations using March CPS data.

sources to the total value. Table 1-2 shows the share of total household income generated by each of five sources of income by population group. For comparison, the table includes the values for the entire working-age population. The household incomes of working-age persons overwhelmingly come from the labor earnings of the working-age person or other members of the household. Over the entire period, less than 13 percent of household income came from SSDI/SSI and public transfers combined, and less than 10 percent came from all other income. Consistent with the earnings rates shown in table 1-1, the "own earnings" contribution to household income of working-age men with disabilities fell from 23 percent in 1982 to just over 12 percent in 2009, while the contribution of SSDI/SSI payments rose from 14 percent in 1982 to just over 25.4 percent in 2009. The labor-earnings contribution to

TABLE 1-2
SHARE OF TOTAL HOUSEHOLD INCOME BY SOURCE FOR
VULNERABLE WORKING-AGE PERSONS, SELECTED YEARS

		Own Labor Income	Others' Labor Income	Own SSI/SSDI	Own Public Assistance	All Other Income
All Working-Age Persons	1982	42.5%	40.6%	1.4%	3.0%	12.5%
	1993	45.0%	39.0%	1.9%	2.5%	11.7%
	2004	45.9%	38.7%	2.4%	1.1%	11.8%
	2009	45.4%	38.8%	2.7%	2.1%	11.0%
Men with Disabilities	1982	23.1%	27.7%	14.0%	11.2%	24.1%
	1993	8.3%	39.8%	18.2%	6.5%	27.2%
	2004	14.4%	29.9%	24.4%	5.8%	25.5%
	2009	12.2%	31.4%	25.4%	6.0%	25.1%
Women with Disabilities	1982	10.9%	42.3%	12.9%	8.8%	25.2%
	1993	13.7%	35.8%	18.3%	2.6%	29.6%
	2004	8.4%	39.3%	23.8%	4.1%	24.4%
	2009	9.6%	33.8%	27.0%	3.9%	25.7%
Single Mothers	1982	45.4%	13.5%	4.8%	20.6%	15.7%
	1993	45.9%	14.7%	5.5%	18.0%	15.9%
	2004	56.1%	17.7%	4.8%	4.8%	16.7%
	2009	53.3%	18.9%	5.4%	5.5%	16.9%

SOURCE: Authors' calculations using March CPS data.
NOTE: All values are based on means; share = mean (income from source / mean household income).

household income for working-age women with disabilities also fell over the period, from about 11 percent in 1982 to about 9.6 percent in 2009. The contribution of SSDI/SSI transfers increased from about 13 percent to 27 percent. The data for single mothers again stand apart from those of people with disabilities. The contribution of single mothers' own earnings rose over the period, from 45 percent in 1982 to 53 percent in 2009 (although this is a drop from a peak of 56 percent in 2004). As their earnings contribution rose, the share of their household income contributed by their own public transfers fell from about 21 percent in 1982 to 5.5 percent in 2009.

A closer look at the data shows that employment is a key reason for the differences in the sources of income among these groups. Figure 1-4

FIGURE 1-4

EMPLOYMENT RATES OF WORKING-AGE POPULATIONS OVER TIME

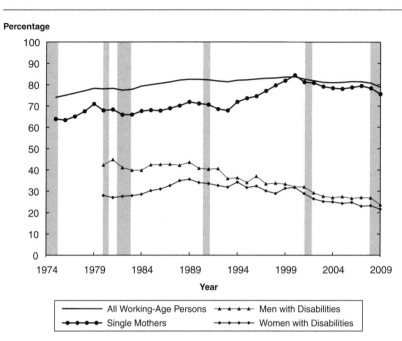

SOURCE: Authors' calculations using March CPS data.
NOTE: Gray bars denote NBER recessions.

plots trends in employment among all working-age people, men and women with disabilities, and single mothers from 1974 through 2009.[9] While there is some variation within business cycles, about 80 percent of the working-age population is employed generally. Single mothers consistently have employment rates above those of men or women with disabilities, but employment rates for single mothers moved very little over the 1980s business cycle. They increased only slightly, from 65.9 percent in 1982 to 67.9 percent in 1993. Over this same period, the employment rate of men with disabilities drifted downward from 41.1 percent to 35.9 percent, and the employment rate of women with disabilities rose slightly from 27.6 percent to 31.9. Beginning in 1993 and especially between 1996 and 2000, however, the employment rate of single mothers grew substantially, increasing to 78.4 percent in 2004.

FIGURE 1-5
AVERAGE MONTHLY WAGES OF TOTAL WORKING-AGE POPULATION
AND AVERAGE VALUE OF SSDI AND SSI BENEFIT PAYMENTS OVER TIME

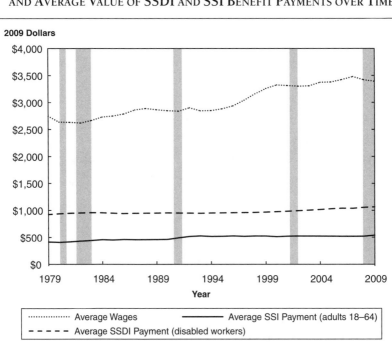

SOURCE: Social Security Administration, various years.
NOTE: Gray bars denote NBER recessions.

Since 1999, the gap between employment rates for single mothers and the overall rate of the working-age population has nearly been closed. Although employment rates for single mothers have come down in the recent recession, they have neither dropped precipitously nor declined disproportionately relative to the declines in rates for all working-age people. In contrast, the employment rates of both men and women with disabilities dropped substantially after 1993 and were at 24 and 22 percent, respectively, in 2009. In both cases, these percentages are lower than their employment rates in 1982.

These simple tables and figures highlight the very different experiences of single mothers and people with disabilities over the past two decades. For single mothers, employment rates and household income rose. For individuals with disabilities, the picture was completely different. Over the past fifteen years, household size–adjusted income for men and women with disabilities grew much less quickly than that of the total working-age population or single mothers. At the same time, employment rates declined and benefit receipts rose for men and women with disabilities. Figure 1-5 shows why this substitution of benefits for earnings did not work well for people with disabilities. The figure plots the average value of SSI and SSDI benefits with the average wage for the entire working-age population in real terms from 1979 through 2009. Although the gap between benefits and wages is always large, it grew considerably after 1996 as productivity and the returns to work rose. Thus, despite considerable increases in public expenditures on those with disabilities, their economic well-being has changed little.

Summary

The data in this chapter highlight three important points related to the themes presented in this book. First, the design of public policies targeted at different groups matters for the outcomes we observe. When programs are designed to award cash transfers in lieu of work, employment falls. When programs are designed to encourage work and award transfers only when work clearly is not possible, employment rises. Second, participation in the labor market generally leads to increased income. As we will show in chapter 2, this is especially true when public policies make work profitable through certain components of the tax system. Finally, receiving public cash transfers in the United States, such as SSDI and SSI, comes with a cost; the price is limited income growth that, over time, leaves recipients further and further behind the rest of the population.

2

Lessons from Welfare Reform

The results in chapter 1 showed that the shift from cash-based benefits under Aid to Families with Dependent Children to employment-based support under Temporary Assistance for Needy Families improved the relative economic status of single mothers and demonstrated how their outcomes differed from those of men and women with disabilities. In this chapter, we briefly discuss AFDC and TANF and how the 1996 welfare reforms changed incentives such that single mothers, state and local administrators, and others began to look to employment over cash benefits as a primary means of support for eligible families. We also discuss how changes in the Earned Income Tax Credit (EITC) and other in-kind benefits contributed to making employment possible and profitable for these women. This chapter is meant to highlight the aspects of welfare reform that might inform changes in disability policy. For a thorough treatment of welfare reform and the empirical evidence regarding its success and failures, see GAO (2010a), Moffitt (2008), and Blank (2007).

AFDC: Goals and Outcomes

The Social Security Act created the Aid to Dependent Children program in 1935. The program's original intent was to insure low-income women with children against negative economic shocks—particularly those associated with widowhood—by providing them with financial assistance such that they could remain out of the labor force and at home with their children. Later renamed Aid to Families with Dependent Children, this categorical federal entitlement program provided aid to children in low-income, usually single-parent families that satisfied certain income and asset requirements.

The original intentions of AFDC influenced program design at both the federal and state levels. Since AFDC was designed for low-income mothers who were not expected to work, most states reduced benefits to these families by one dollar for every dollar earned (a 100 percent benefit-reduction rate), all but eliminating incentives to work. Since these mothers were not seen as able to obtain heath insurance or other forms of support through employers, over time AFDC became linked with a range of other programs, including Medicaid and food stamps.

As long as most AFDC participants were widows and most women with children (married or otherwise) were not working, the program attracted little negative attention. However, as figure 2-1 shows, the foundation underlying AFDC began to shift in the 1960s. The figure shows

FIGURE 2-1

PERCENTAGE OF NEVER-MARRIED SINGLE MOTHERS RECEIVING AFDC
AND MOTHERS NOT IN THE LABOR FORCE, SELECTED YEARS

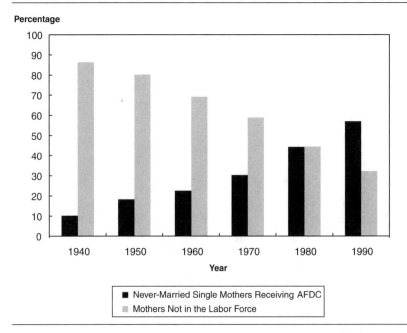

SOURCE: U.S. Department of Health and Human Services (DHHS) 2008; Integrated Public Use Microdata Series 2010.

the percentage of women with children not participating in the labor market (working or looking for work) as well as the percentage of AFDC caseloads occupied by never-married women with children. By the late 1960s, women with children were increasingly in, rather than out of, the labor force and a growing number of AFDC recipients had never been married. These trends raised questions about the legitimacy of continuing AFDC.[1]

Over time these concerns developed into a series of debates and policy changes meant to regain control over AFDC caseloads. For nearly two decades, prior to welfare reform, the federal government supported state-managed experiments designed to induce women to leave welfare for work (Moffitt 2003; Blank 2002). These experiments included financial incentives, small-scale work programs, job training and education

FIGURE 2-2

PERCENTAGE OF FAMILIES RECEIVING AFDC/TANF BENEFITS AND PERCENTAGE OF WELFARE-DEPENDENT WORKING-AGE SINGLE MOTHERS OVER TIME

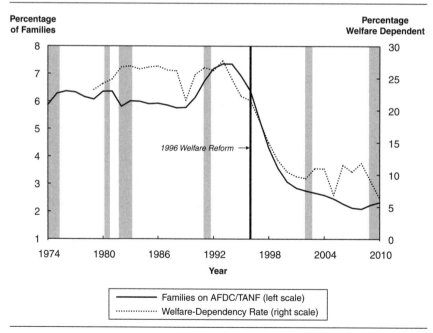

SOURCE: U.S. DHHS 2008; authors' calculations using March CPS data.
NOTE: Gray bars denote NBER recessions.

programs, and various small-scale state mandates on individuals to induce them to try work.[2] None of these programs proved very successful at moving existing AFDC recipients off welfare and into work. The reforms also did little to stem the flow of new entrants to the program, so caseloads continued to increase. Social scientists' evaluation of these experiments provided little convincing evidence that AFDC caseloads or expenditures could be controlled through partial adjustments to the existing eligibility and benefit structure.

While much of the focus was on controlling caseloads and costs, the impact of AFDC on single women also brought disappointing news. Figure 2-2 shows a measure of welfare dependence defined by the U.S. Department of Health and Human Services (DHHS) in its annual report to Congress. Families receiving more than half of their total family income in one year from AFDC/TANF, food stamps, or SSI are considered welfare dependent (U.S. DHHS 2008). As the figure shows, even in periods of relatively modest caseload growth, welfare-dependency rates were rising among single mothers.

From AFDC to TANF

In the early 1990s, the idea that prior AFDC reforms were ineffective was joined with a growing public interest in personal responsibility and work alternatives to welfare. At the same time, interest in states' rights was increasing, and states became resistant to unfunded federal mandates. Together these factors prompted states to formally ask the federal government for permission to run much broader and more innovative welfare experiments. These permissions, known as waivers, allowed states to depart from federally administered eligibility criteria and to use federal and state funds to experiment with alternative ways of supporting AFDC-eligible mothers. Forty-three states obtained waivers at some point between 1993 and 1996 (CEA 1997). States used the waivers to experiment with alternative welfare-delivery structures, including strict work requirements without allowances for school attendance, sanctions or the removal or limitation of benefits after a prescribed time period, reduction of marginal tax rates similar to a negative income tax, and family caps on benefits (that is, not

FIGURE 2-3

DESCRIPTION OF GOVERNMENT ASSISTANCE FOR NEEDY FAMILIES BEFORE AND AFTER THE 1996 WELFARE REFORM

BEFORE

AFDC
(AID TO FAMILIES WITH DEPENDENT CHILDREN)

Financing: States annually entitled to unlimited federal funds for reimbursement of benefit payments, at "matching" rates inversely related to state per-capita income.

Eligibility: Children deprived of support of one parent or children in low-income two-parent families (AFDC-UP). Income and asset limits apply.

State Requirements: States required to provide aid, almost exclusively in the form of cash payments, to all persons who meet state and federal eligibility requirements. Under the Job Opportunities and Basic Skills (JOBS) program created in 1988, states were required to have a specified percentage of their caseloads participating in JOBS activities, which included education and training.

Individual Requirements: Individuals received benefits as long as they met eligibility requirements. No time limit for receiving benefits.

Interaction with Other Programs: AFDC eligibility guaranteed Medicaid and food stamps eligibility.

WELFARE
REFORM
1996

AFTER

TANF
(TEMPORARY ASSISTANCE FOR NEEDY FAMILIES)

Financing: States annually receive a fixed block grant from the federal government reflecting AFDC expenditures from 1992 to 1995.

Eligibility: Children in low-income families as designated by state; AFDC-UP abolished.

State Requirements: Spending required to conform to federally-determined goals and states are required to achieve annual beneficiary employment targets, but benefit levels, income and asset limits, and treatment of earnings disregards are left to the states' discretion. States are free to use funds for services and noncash benefits.

Individual Requirements: Individuals may receive benefits for a maximum of five years, but states may exempt up to 20 percent of their caseload. Beneficiaries must be engaged in specified work activities (which generally exclude education) within two years of receiving benefits in order to continue to qualify.

Interaction with Other Programs: TANF eligibility decoupled from Medicaid and food stamps eligibility.

SOURCE: U.S. DHHS 2009; Ruggles 1998; and Burke 1996.

awarding additional money for any number of children greater than the cap), among others. These experiments produced an array of new data and showed, over many states and various structures, that revamping the system, rather than simply modifying some of its elements, could yield large benefits.

Welfare reform was passed at the federal level in 1996. It gave the states control of federal welfare funds while making that funding contingent on complying with many of the program-design lessons learned through the state-waiver system. Figure 2-3 shows the changes from AFDC to TANF and discusses the key elements associated with these changes. For a more complete discussion of both the path to welfare reform and the changes it brought, see Haskins (2006a), Ellwood (2003), and Blank and Ellwood (2002).

Elements of Welfare Reform

The welfare-reform legislation converted the AFDC federal matching grant to a federal block grant and removed most of the federal authority over its use. As such, states became free to design their own programs, which included setting benefit levels, tax rates, income limits, and asset requirements. Additionally, states were allowed to use TANF funds to provide cash assistance or to fund in-kind services such as child care, job training, job search support, and social services. There were no limitations or mandates dictating how or when the federal funds were to be spent. States could expand the types of families they covered and, importantly, were not required to cover specific groups or all of those meeting federal eligibility criteria. Unlike AFDC, TANF was not an open-ended transfer program; rather, it was a federal commitment to a fixed level of funds for state use in assisting state-defined needy populations.

In lieu of federal authority over state-program design, the federal government imposed national standards on the amount of time any adult could receive benefits. Federal funds came with a clear restriction on lifetime use. Individuals were not allowed to receive federal TANF funds for more than sixty months in their lifetime, although states were allowed to exempt 20 percent of their annual caseload from this requirement. In addition to time limits on benefit receipt, federal block grants were contingent on state enforcement of federally imposed work requirements. Under the reforms, 50 percent of states' overall caseload had to be working by 2002, and 90 percent of states' two-parent caseload had to be working by 1999. Departing substantially from prior reforms, general education (such as GED [general educational development] studies) and job-training programs generally could *not* be counted as work. Finally, the required number of hours spent working made it clear that work requirements were meant to be serious attachments to the labor market: single mothers were required to work thirty hours per week by 2000, and the combined work hours of two-parent families had to average thirty-five hours per week.

In response to the creation of TANF, states implemented more work-focused welfare programs. In several informative studies, the Government Accountability Office (GAO 1998, 2001, 2010a) shows that the states focused on helping low-income parents find jobs and converted welfare offices into job-placement service centers. States also expanded opportunities for parents to work and receive benefits. Along with incentives to work, states imposed financial consequences, or sanctions, on families that did not comply with TANF work or other requirements. According to the GAO (2010a), these changes the states made—along with the expansion of the EITC, federal money to support child care, and good economic conditions—helped raise the incomes of single-parent families, moving them beyond the income threshold required for cash assistance.

Although not all low-income single-parent families moved into work and off of cash benefits, the ability of the welfare reforms to reduce caseloads without increasing poverty rates among single mothers is generally considered a success. A key contributor to the positive outcome was the early recognition that work incentives must be accompanied by economic profitability for the targeted population. Thus, enhancements to the EITC and new allowances to the Medicaid program (such as the State Children's Health Insurance Program [SCHIP]), as well as the Child Tax Credit, child care subsidies, and job training, were essential to the observed success of the program. These expansions were not without costs; in fact expenditures on single-mother families changed little following welfare reform (Haskins 2006a). However, TANF allowed states flexibility in the way they provided services to their citizens, which enabled the states, to an extent, to move part of their low-income populations into work and to take advantage of federally funded programs to boost benefit recipients' earnings and help them with their health care costs.

Changing Incentives

The 1996 welfare reform not only changed the rules and regulations governing funding and benefit distribution but, as seen in figure 2-4a, it also changed the incentives individuals and states faced when deciding

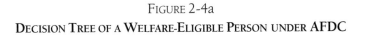

FIGURE 2-4a
DECISION TREE OF A WELFARE-ELIGIBLE PERSON UNDER AFDC

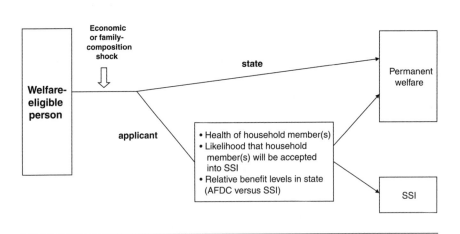

SOURCE: Authors' description of the decision-making process.

how best to manage economic shocks. This component of the reforms is the most relevant for thinking about disability policy. As the figure shows, under the AFDC system, individuals experiencing an economic or family composition change that made them eligible for AFDC put in their application and waited to be accepted or not accepted in the program.

FIGURE 2-4b
DECISION TREE OF A WELFARE-ELIGIBLE PERSON UNDER TANF

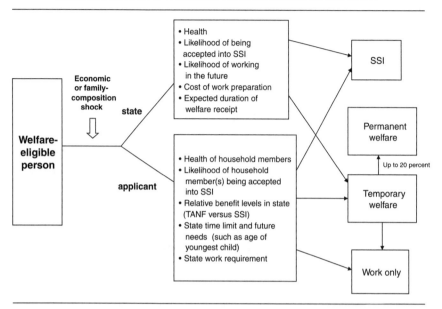

SOURCE: Authors' description of the decision-making process.

Other than modest attempts at imposing job training, education, or job-search requirements, single-mother applicants were principally screened on the basis of their family structure and income. Those who met the criteria for eligibility were granted access to benefits. States had little reason to restrict access, since the federal government gave matching grants for caseload increases.

Moreover, to the extent that single mothers applying for AFDC faced challenges to employment associated with low education or limited job experience, their incentives to shift from the certainty of benefits and health care and other in-kind transfers to the uncertainty of work that might originally pay less than AFDC were not high. In these cases, state gatekeepers might also have worried about the well-being of less-skilled single mothers who were pushed off AFDC and back into the labor market. This was especially the case since states were not bearing the full cost of maintaining these women and their families on AFDC. Given these reasons, it is not surprising that there was little movement off the rolls before welfare reform.

Figure 2-4b shows how TANF altered these incentives. TANF changed the incentives for individuals and states. Through lifetime limits and work requirements, TANF effectively raised the costs of receiving benefits, and by making work profitable through expansions to the EITC, it increased the benefits of work. This changed the calculation for single mothers to one in which investing in work earned a higher return than investing in benefit receipt.[3] Similarly, states' incentives changed under the reforms. Since states were forced to count each nonworking beneficiary against their caseload requirements, they had incentives to direct single mothers to the workplace as quickly and intensively as possible. Low-income residents who states effectively moved to work could then gain access to federal income support through the EITC and to health care through federally subsidized Medicaid benefits.

An additional major feature of welfare reform was the shift of funds to the states via fixed or so-called block grants. Block grants were based on the state caseloads between 1992 and 1996 and held constant in nominal terms. The states were able to use any savings from reduced expenditures to fund alternative work-based programs targeted at single mothers and to help other families in need. The ability to keep these program savings gave states an additional financial incentive to focus more resources on work-support programs, such as child care.

Measuring Success

As shown in chapter 1 and in figure 2-2, caseloads dropped rapidly following welfare reform and stayed far below their prereform levels even during the 2001–2002 recession and through 2010, the latest year of data available. At the same time, the welfare-dependency rate of single mothers fell (see figure 2-2), while single mothers' employment and income rose (see the figures in chapter 1). Research suggests that welfare reform reduced transfer caseloads and increased single mothers' employment without increasing their poverty rates or lowering their average household income (Blank 2002; Meyer 2010; Meyer and Rosenbaum 2000).[4] Meyer and

Sullivan (2008) show that both mean consumption and household income increased in 1993–95 and 1997–2000 for single mothers.

The consensus seems to be that labor-force participation and employment increased as a result of the reforms. Among women who left welfare, employment rates ranged from 60 to 70 percent; employment rates for women continuing on welfare rose from less than 10 percent to more than 30 percent (Moffitt 2008). Research from the Congressional Budget Office (CBO 2007) shows that as employment rose, the composition of income for single mothers also changed, tilting away from cash benefits and toward earnings and the EITC (see figure 2-5). Overall, most studies found positive net effects on earnings, increases in average family income,

FIGURE 2-5

INCOME OF FEMALE-HEADED, LOW-INCOME HOUSEHOLDS
WITH CHILDREN BY SOURCE, OVER TIME

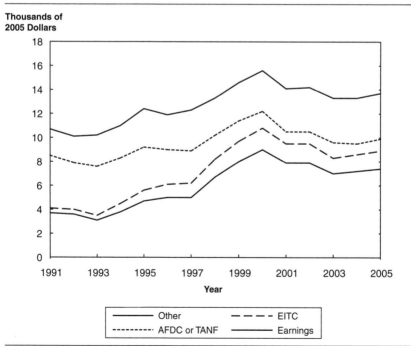

SOURCE: Congressional Budget Office 2007.

and declines in poverty rates (Blank 2002). These data suggest that the low employment levels achieved by single mothers under AFDC were in part reflective of the work incentives (or lack thereof) in the welfare system. Under TANF, the average single mother became employed and, with the subsidies provided by the EITC, able to maintain her household income at a higher level than under AFDC.

Of course, the reforms did not result in the removal of all single mothers from cash-assistance programs. For those unable to work, states continued to provide cash benefits. States also provided cash benefits to those who were able to work but not at a self-sufficient level. Blank and Kovak (2008) find that those who did stay on the rolls make up a heterogeneous group. About 50–55 percent of this group consists of short- and long-term recipients with sufficiently low hours or wages to qualify for TANF cash payments and families that use the program for short-term spells of economic disruption. The remaining 40–45 percent of the caseload consists of long-term recipients who are not working or are working sporadically. These individuals continue to be largely dependent on cash-transfer programs.

That not everyone previously on AFDC could leave the rolls and enter employment and that about half of those currently qualified for TANF cash benefits are long-term recipients is not surprising. It reflects the fact that there are working-age individuals who, for myriad reasons, are unable to work in the labor market even when given reasonable incentives and support. For those individuals, cash assistance may be the best way to ensure that they can maintain their households. Alternatively, as Blank and Kovak (2008) suggest, we could create special programs for these individuals that provide more intensive employment supports than those available to the average person. An important lesson from this, however, is that by making work the default and aligning incentives and supports to encourage people to seek employment over benefits, policies can reduce the pressure on administrators to contain growth in the rolls. The people who remain on the rolls under the reformed welfare system are more likely unable to work in the labor market and in need of cash-benefit support.

Lessons for Reforming Disability Policy

Welfare reform provides one example of how a long-standing policy can be changed and how the changes can lead to shifts in individual and institutional behavior. A critical lesson from welfare reform is that many people who were receiving benefits were able, with reasonable levels of support, to find employment. Despite multiple hurdles—such as low education levels, limited skills, and little job experience—single mothers' employment increased following welfare reform. Not surprisingly, a subset of single mothers unable to successfully transition from welfare to work remains, but this is a small portion of the single mothers previously on AFDC. Importantly, it is also a group that, by demonstration rather than assumption, is unable to integrate effectively into the labor market even with appropriate incentives and support. This offers an important advantage over categorical programs that can expand in unintended ways when individuals are able to change their behavior to become eligible, for example, by becoming single mothers or claiming that a disability makes them unable to work.

Another important lesson from the caseload data is that welfare reform discouraged entry as much as it encouraged exit. This result is likely due to a number of factors, including the announcement that permanent welfare benefits were no longer available; the incentives placed on states to make work a priority; and the access to benefits that made work possible and advantageous for single mothers, such as work-related access to child-care credits and the EITC.[5] This suggests that a work-first strategy, combined with work-based support, can be important for motivating individuals to move into the labor market.

Turning to the process of changing legislation, the twenty years of generally unsuccessful attempts to give AFDC beneficiaries incentives to work by making only minor adjustments to tax rates and employment disincentives highlights the difficulties of this approach. Meaningful changes to the program began only when states, through waivers, were allowed to try a range of approaches that included incentives and penalties to refocus the attention of individuals and state administrators on work. The state-waiver process provides another important lesson: experimentation and data collection at the state level greatly improve our understanding of the incentives that matter and increase the chances that large federal policy changes will work. This data collection and period of trial and error should not be undervalued. It provided policymakers with evidence of what was required to be successful and of what could work if implemented. The waiver period also produced a set of "best practices" states could learn from when deciding how to set up their own TANF programs. Finally, the process of experimentation at the state level highlighted the opportunity to devolve these welfare programs to the states. This devolution of responsibilities and funding gave states the incentive to make work a priority.

Summary

The lessons from the 1996 welfare reforms inform our thoughts on disability policy and potential reforms. The key message for disability policy is that many disability beneficiaries may also have had greater potential for work than the outcomes observed under current cash-benefit programs demonstrate. Uncovering the potential for work among any population is made easier when policies prioritize work and require that applicants make attempts to work before being considered for nonwork-related benefits.

3

The Adult Disability Determination Process and Growing Adult Disability Rolls

As previous chapters have shown, the two major cash-transfer programs targeted at working-age people with disabilities—Social Security Disability Insurance and Supplemental Security Income—grew substantially over the past two decades with respect to both total costs and number of beneficiaries. Figure 3-1 provides a more complete look at how these trends have evolved by plotting the importance of disability programs relative to the active working-age population from 1970 through 2010.[1] Relative importance is defined as the number of Americans receiving disability transfer benefits (SSDI and SSI) per thousand employed persons of active working age in the United States. As the figure indicates, the U.S. caseload-per-worker ratio has grown substantially since 1970. Moreover, it has fluctuated over time; program growth was rapid in the 1970s, followed by relatively slow growth over the 1980s and relatively rapid growth thereafter.

There are three possible explanations for this growth pattern: changes in the underlying severity of disability in the United States, changes in the eligibility rules for SSDI and SSI program benefits, and changes in the interpretation and implementation of these rules over time.[2] In this chapter we show that policy changes, rather than changes in the underlying health of the working-age population, are the most likely drivers of growth and movement in the disability benefit rolls. We begin by contrasting the fluctuations in program growth in figure 3-1 with the relatively unchanging patterns of severe health conditions in the working-age population. We then discuss the difference between having a severe health-based impairment and being disabled and why recognizing the

FIGURE 3-1

NUMBER OF SSDI AND SSI-DISABLED BENEFICIARIES
PER THOUSAND WORKERS AGES FIFTEEN TO SIXTY-FOUR OVER TIME

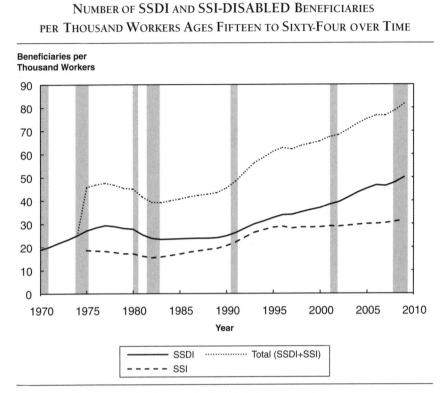

SOURCE: Aarts, Burkhauser, and de Jong 1996, table 1.1; Social Security Administration, various years a;
and International Labour Organization, 1998–2010.
NOTE: Gray bars denote NBER recessions.

potential for divergence between the two is critical for creating effective
and sustainable disability policy. Within this context, we review how U.S.
disability policy has changed over time and link these changes to the
trends portrayed in figure 3-1. We conclude that policy, rather than
health, has driven program growth.

Trends in Health and Work Disability

Before examining how changes in disability program rules might have
influenced benefit growth, it is important to see how much of the growth

and movement in figure 3-1 can be explained by changes in the underlying health of working-age Americans. Although there are excellent administrative data on those receiving federal benefits for disability, data available to track the overall prevalence of poor health and disability among the working-age population are very limited. As such, we must rely on incomplete data from several different sources to develop a picture of the relationship between health and disability and how this relationship has changed over time.

We begin by looking at trends in health status collected in the National Health Interview Survey (NHIS [National Center for Health Statistics 2010]). Figure 3-2a shows trends in the percentage of working-age individuals reporting that they are in fair or poor health by age group. Not surprisingly, the prevalence of fair or poor health is higher for older than for younger people, but, importantly, these percentages have varied little

FIGURE 3-2a

PERCENTAGE OF U.S. RESIDENTS REPORTING FAIR OR POOR HEALTH,
BY AGE GROUP, OVER TIME

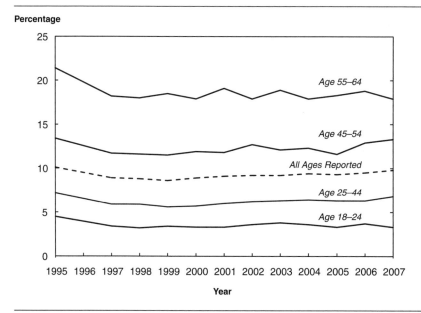

SOURCE: National Center for Health Statistics 2010.

over time for all groups. Over the past ten years the overall prevalence of fair or poor health in the working-age population has remained relatively steady at about 9 percent.

Another way to think about changes in the underlying health or impairment level in the population is to look at how many individuals report that their health limits the amount or type of work they can do. Figure 3-2b, reproduced from Houtenville et al. (2009), uses data from the Current Population Survey to compare the prevalence of work limitations among different age groups in the working-age population. In contrast to the substantial fluctuation in the ratio of caseloads per thousand workers over time in figure 3-1, the prevalence of work limitations among all working-age people remained fairly stable at about 8 percent between 1980 and 2008 with no clearly discernible trend. Like the

FIGURE 3-2b

PERCENTAGE OF U.S. RESIDENTS REPORTING A WORK LIMITATION, BY AGE GROUP, OVER TIME

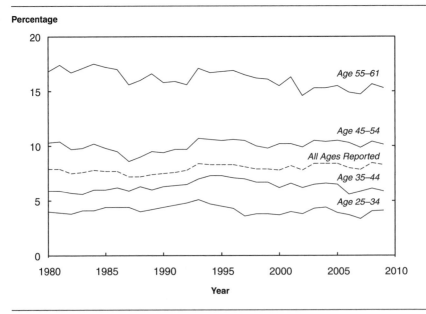

SOURCE: Houtenville et al. 2009, table 5; and authors' calculations using Ma   rch CPS data.

fair- and poor-health measure, the prevalence of work limitations is greater at older ages than at younger ages, but there are no clear trends for any age group over the entire period.

The relative stability of the health data is inconsistent with the idea that an increase in the prevalence of disabilities in the working-age population is responsible for the fluctuations in caseloads per thousand workers found in figure 3-1. The stability seen in the measures of poor health and work limitations supports the view that changes in underlying health are not the principal drivers of disability benefit caseloads over the past three decades.

Defining and Measuring Disability

Although disability is frequently thought of as an immutable, health-based condition that limits functionality and prevents the performance of socially expected tasks (such as attending school, going into the military, or working), neither advocates for those with disabilities nor the data support this idea. A more accurate concept of disability, and one embodied in the Americans with Disabilities Act, considers disability to be the product of an interactive process between an individual's health conditions and social and physical environment. In this perspective, disability is neither immutable nor determined solely by health.

This is the perspective adopted by the World Health Organization's (WHO) International Classification of Functioning, Disability, and Health (ICF). The ICF lists four major concepts in its definition of disability: impairment, activity limitation, participation restriction, and disability (WHO 2001). A prerequisite for each of these concepts is the presence of a health condition (including a disease, injury, health disorder, or other health-related condition). *Impairment* is defined as a significant deviation or loss in body function or structure (for example, paraplegia or reduced vision). *Activity limitation* is defined as difficulty an individual may have in executing activities. For example, a person with paraplegia will have great difficulty walking, and a person with macular degeneration will have great difficulty seeing. A *participation restriction* is defined as a problem that an individual may experience in life situations. For example, a working-age person with such health conditions may have difficulty working, not because of the severity of the impairment, but because of the physical environment (for example, due to a lack of reasonable employer accommodations) or the social environment (such as discrimination or government programs that provide benefits to people with these conditions only if they do not work). In the ICF, the term *disability* means the presence of an impairment, activity limitation, or participation restriction. Figure 3-3 shows that while these concepts can overlap, it is possible for one to occur without the others.

This concept of disability clearly allows for differences among the population with impairments and work limitations, but what do the data say? Table 3-1, reproduced from Burkhauser and Houtenville (2009), uses NHIS data to examine the prevalence of impairments and work

FIGURE 3-3

SIMPLIFIED CONCEPTUAL MODEL OF DISABILITY USING ICF CONCEPTS

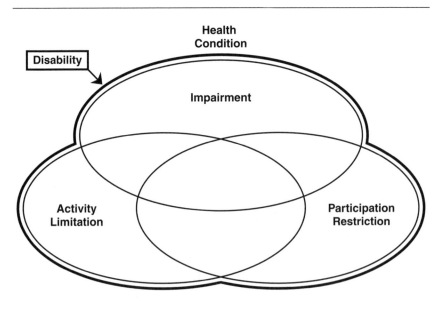

SOURCE: Weathers 2009.

TABLE 3-1
PREVALENCE OF SELECTED IMPAIRMENTS AMONG MEN AGES TWENTY-FIVE
TO SIXTY-ONE AND EMPLOYMENT RATES IN THOSE IMPAIRMENT
POPULATIONS, POOLED OVER SURVEY YEARS 1983–1996[a]

Impairments[b]	Prevalence			Employment Rates		
	All	With Work Limitations	Ratio[d]	All	With Work Limitations	Ratio[d]
One or More of the Following Impairments:	23.4	5.8	0.25	81.5	47.7	0.59
—Visual Impairments	4.8	1.2	0.24	81.2	43.5	0.54
Blind in Both Eyes	0.2	0.1	0.65	49.4	28.1	0.57
Other Visual Impairments	4.7	1.1	0.23	82.4	45.2	0.55
—Hearing Impairments	10.8	2.3	0.22	81.6	44.9	0.55
Deaf in Both Ears	0.5	0.2	0.35	75.4	49.1	0.65
Other Hearing Impairments	10.2	2.1	0.21	81.9	44.5	0.54
—Sensation Impairments[c]	0.5	0.1	0.26	79.9	50.5	0.63
—Speech Impairments	1.0	0.5	0.47	61.7	30.1	0.49
Stammering and Stuttering	0.6	0.2	0.32	70.2	28.3	0.40
Other Speech Impairments.	0.4	0.3	0.69	48.6	31.4	0.65
—Paralysis	0.4	0.3	0.87	32.2	26.4	0.82
Paraplegia, Hemiplegia, or Quadriplegia	0.2	0.2	0.95	22.3	21.8	0.98
Paraparesis, Hemiparesis	0.1	0.1	0.91	25.3	23.7	0.94
Cerebral Palsy	0.1	0.1	0.68	58.3	43.7	0.75
—Absence of One or Both Legs	0.1	0.1	0.77	34.2	27.8	0.81
—Deformity/Orthopedic Impairments	10.0	3.0	0.30	81.1	52.6	0.65
Back/Spine	8.7	2.5	0.29	81.4	51.8	0.64
Shoulder(s)	1.8	0.7	0.40	76.4	52.6	0.69
—Mental Retardation	0.5	0.4	0.88	34.6	32.8	0.95

SOURCE: Adapted from Burkhauser and Houtenville 2009, tables 8 and 9.
NOTES:
a. People are considered to have a work limitation if they have any impairments or health problems that keep them from working at a job or business or that limit them in the kind or amount of work they can do. Only individuals who were directly asked about these impairments are included, which is approximately one-sixth of the NHIS sample in each year. Cells with sample sizes of fewer than thirty respondents are not reported.
b. Category terms are based on the language of the survey. Individuals may report more than one impairment; hence, the table rows may contain multiple observations of the same respondent.
c. Sensation impairments include impairments in taste, smell, and loss or disturbance of sensation and numbness of any body part.
d. The ratio of column 2 (5) to column 1 (4). When these ratios were calculated, four decimal points were allowed in the components of the ratios.

limitations among the working-age population.[3] Column 1 of table 3-1 shows the percentage of working-age men who report having one of the impairments in the list, the percentage who report having both an impairment and a work limitation, and the ratio of the two.[4] As row 1 shows, while about one-quarter of working-age men report one of the impairments listed, fewer than 6 percent report a work limitation. This means just 25 percent of men reporting one or more impairments also report having a work limitation. A similar story holds for women (not shown). These data show that a majority of both working-age men and women with impairments do not report a work limitation.

The percentage of those with an impairment who also report a work limitation also varies substantially across impairment groups. While around 90 percent of men with paraplegia, hemiplegia, or quadriplegia; paraparesis or hemiparesis; and mental retardation report a work limitation, the impairment with the next highest rate of work limitation, missing one or both legs, drops to 77 percent. While 35 percent of men who are deaf in both ears and 65 percent of men who are blind in both eyes report a work limitation, only around 20 percent of those who have other hearing or visual impairments report a work limitation. The share of women (not shown) reporting a work limitation in these impairment categories is similar.

The remaining columns in the table show the variation in employment rates across men reporting an impairment versus those reporting an impairment *and* a work limitation. The data point to important differences. While the employment rate of working-age men with an impairment *and* a work limitation is 47.7 percent, the employment rate of the entire working-age population with impairments is far higher, 81.5 percent. Not surprisingly, this difference varies by impairment classification. For example, among men with paraplegia, hemiplegia, and quadriplegia or paraparesis or hemiparesis, employment rates are about the same for those who do and do not report a work limitation. In contrast, for those with deformity/orthopedic and visual and hearing impairments, those who report a work limitation are much less likely to be employed than those who do not.

We interpret these data as confirmation of the insights embodied by the ADA and in the ICF definition: there is not a perfect correlation between severity of impairment and ability to work, and the determinants of work ability are frequently related to the social and physical environments in which an individual operates. Unfortunately, the concept that social and environmental factors—including the incentives and constraints embedded in benefit programs—might influence the work and benefit decisions of those with health conditions has yet to influence material changes in U.S. disability policy.[5] In the following discussion of U.S. disability policy, we show how failing to integrate these insights into policy has contributed to the rapid increase in disability caseloads over the past two decades.

FIGURE 3-4

SSDI APPLICATIONS AND THE UNEMPLOYMENT RATE OVER TIME

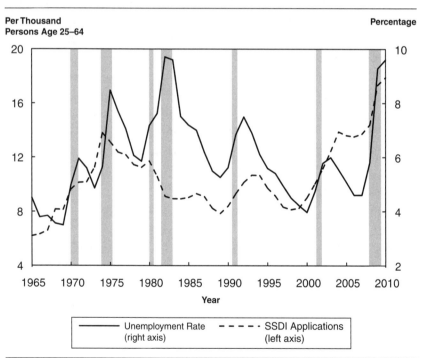

SOURCE: Duggan and Imberman 2008, figure 11.5; SSA 2010b; U.S. Department of Commerce, Bureau of the Census; and U.S. Bureau of Labor Statistics, 2011.
NOTE: Gray bars denote NBER recessions.

Other Drivers of Disability Caseloads

If health and disability are not the primary drivers of caseload growth, what other factors might be important? One answer is the economy. There is a significant body of literature documenting how the business cycle affects caseloads. Figure 3-4, which traces the SSDI application rate and the national unemployment rate from 1965 through 2010, shows that, with the exception of the double-dip recession of the early 1980s, application rates are highly correlated with the business cycle; they rise during recessions and fall during periods of economic growth. Another factor driving caseload growth is policy, specifically, changes in the rules governing the definition and measurement of disability. Because they can be different, we treat changes in policy and changes in the administration of policy separately here.[6]

Changes in Disability Program Rules. It is by now fairly well understood that changes in program rules over time have affected the growth in caseloads shown in figure 3-1. Here we review the most important program changes and link them back to the fluctuations in caseloads shown in the figure.

The first important change in disability policy, highlighted in figure 3-1, was the introduction of the SSI program in 1974. SSI federalized state programs for the blind and disabled and, in most states, increased benefits available to recipients. SSDI also grew substantially over the first part of the 1970s, as the percentage of lost earnings replaced by SSDI income grew.[7] In the late 1970s, caseloads per worker began to fall in response to changes in the administration of rules. In 1980, Congress required the Social Security Administration to reevaluate all current recipients to see if they still met the medical standards. This rule change resulted in a drop in the SSDI/SSI rolls per thousand workers.[8]

By 1983, the widespread reevaluation of those already on disability rolls was halted as the courts and then Congress restricted the SSA's power to reevaluate beneficiaries. These restrictions required the SSA to demonstrate that a current beneficiary no longer met the original standard for eligibility and that the reason was a significant improvement in the beneficiary's medically based impairment. Passage of this much stricter test all but stopped the removal of beneficiaries from the rolls, provided their work effort did not exceed the substantial gainful activity limit. At the

same time, congressional mandates required the SSA to revise its evaluation of mental illness. This resulted in an expansion of the eligibility
standard for mental illness in 1986. While the impact of this change in
the medical-listing criteria for mental illness was not immediate, its
importance can be seen in the rise in caseloads in later years.[9]

The next set of disability policy changes primarily affected children.
In 1990, the Supreme Court required the SSA to broaden the eligibility
criteria for childhood disability such that adults and children were treated
equally in determining disability. Prior to the *Sullivan v. Zebley* decision,
children who did not meet the medical listing were not eligible for
benefits under any circumstances. This was not the case for adults, who
could qualify on either medical listings or vocational criteria. Thus, *Zebley*
required that the SSA establish a set of age-appropriate "functional criteria"
equivalent to the vocational criteria for adults. This change in the criteria
led to the rapid growth in the SSI-disabled children program in the early
1990s, shown in figure 3-1.

This rapid growth resulted in a final set of program changes that
occurred as part of the 1996 welfare reforms. In response to rapid SSI-
caseload growth and a growing concern that the disability determination
process was allowing too many children without serious medical
problems onto the disability rolls, Congress narrowed the criteria for
childhood disability in 1996. In addition, Congress mandated that the
SSA reevaluate the eligibility of children on the rolls who might not meet
the new eligibility criteria because they received benefits on the basis of
the former, more lenient, standards. As a result, the SSI caseload of disabled children per thousand workers has been relatively constant since
1996; growth in total caseloads has been driven more by increases in the
SSDI caseload.[10]

Changes in the Administration of Disability Program Rules. In addition
to the variation in caseloads associated with changes in the disability
program rules, there have been changes in the principal criteria used to
implement these rules. To get a sense of how implementation can differ
over time, it is useful to look more closely at the disability determination
process. This process is described in detail in box 3-1 on page 49.

The initial disability determination process for both SSDI and SSI incorporates some of the reasoning captured in the ICF disability definition. The SSA defines adult disability as an inability to engage in any substantial gainful activity because of a medically determinable physical or mental impairment that can be expected to result in death or has lasted or can be expected to last for a continuous period of not less than twelve months. Applicants for disability benefits move through a multistep process in which their health-based impairments and the degree to which these impairments affect their ability to work are gauged. This process of determining whether an applicant is eligible for benefits has several layers. The first criterion for denial—the earnings test—is factually easy to establish. While the level of earnings is somewhat arbitrary, it is easy to

FIGURE 3-5

SSA DISABILITY DETERMINATION PROCESS FOR ADULTS, 2000

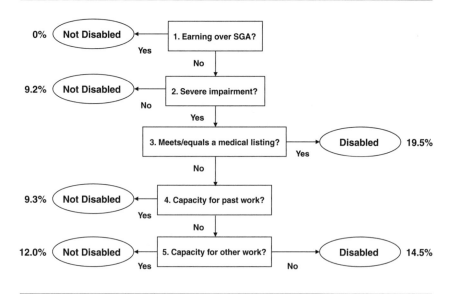

SOURCE: SSA, various years b; SSA 2009a; SSA 2009b.
NOTE: Some percentages are not represented in the figure. These include 17.8 percent that are determined disabled and 7.4 percent that are determined not disabled for "other reasons" for whicl basis of determination is not available; a further 10.3 percent are denied for nonmedical reasons.

verify whether a person is working and earning above the limit. Virtually no one is denied benefits based on this criterion. The next stage is more difficult. Determining whether the applicant's impairment is sufficient to prevent the applicant from working is a key challenge for any disability program. Setting the level of severity too low turns disability programs into long-term benefit programs—unemployment insurance in the case of SSDI and a universal income guarantee in the case of SSI. Conversely, setting the level too high prevents those whose medically based impairments make them unable to work from receiving benefits—an outcome at odds with the purpose of the program. The SSA attempts to set the level of severity (the next two steps in figure 3-5) according to current medical research on the condition in question.[11]

Unfortunately, there is no single answer about the effect most impairments will have on work ability. The work limitations associated with impairments vary by individual and by the social and physical environments in place. Some impairments are easier to judge than others, but where it is more difficult to establish the severity of an impairment or its potential effect on an applicant's ability to work, administrative discretion plays a greater role in determining the applicant's outcome.

To understand the difficulties in judging severity-influenced caseloads, it is useful to look at two of the hard-to-measure impairments: mental illness and musculoskeletal conditions.[12] Figure 3-6 shows the percentage of new SSDI awardees based on mental conditions and musculoskeletal conditions each year between 1967 and 2009. As the figure shows, the share of new beneficiaries who gain eligibility because of these conditions has increased notably over time. In 1967, approximately 20 percent of new beneficiaries had either mental illness or a musculoskeletal condition. By 2009, more than half of all new beneficiaries had one of these conditions. Part of the explanation for this increase is a specific change in the eligibility criteria. This is evident in the rapid rise in the share of new beneficiaries with a mental illness between 1983 and 1986, as the backlog of those removed from SSDI in the early 1980s and those denied entry under the old mental-illness criteria joined the rolls. It is important to note that once that backlog ended in 1987, the share of new beneficiaries who qualified because of a mental illness did not drop to pre-1980 rates but remained at a much higher level. The same pattern can be seen in the

FIGURE 3-6

PERCENTAGE OF SSDI BENEFITS AWARDED FOR MENTAL AND
MUSCULOSKELETAL CONDITIONS OVER TIME

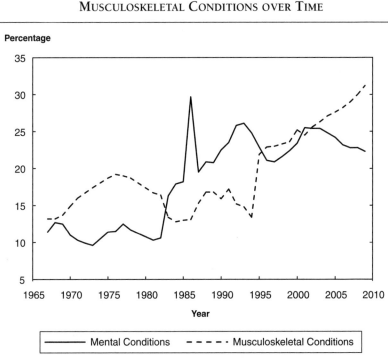

SOURCE: SSA 2009b.

share of new beneficiaries with musculoskeletal conditions. This share rose rapidly in the 1970s, declined in importance when program standards were tightened in the early 1980s, and has reached much higher levels since 1995 than its previous highs in the 1970s.

Another sign that administrative discretion has increased is the growing use of the next step, vocational criteria, in the initial disability determination process described in box 3-1. For applicants who do not meet or exceed the medical listings, program administrators consider a set of vocational criteria. While these criteria have not changed over the history of the SSDI program, their use as qualifying criteria for benefit receipt has risen. Administrative liberalization for determining eligibility for SSI and SSDI played a role in the increase in caseloads for both programs during

Box 3-1: SSA Disability Screening for Adults. The SSA defines adult disability as the inability to engage in substantial gainful activity by reason of a medically determinable physical or mental impairment that is expected to result in death or last at least twelve months. Applicants must be unable to do any work that exists in the national economy for which they are qualified by virtue of age, education, and work experience. The United States does not award federal disability benefits for partial disability.

As a practical matter, the SSA asks the state disability determination offices to follow a five-step procedure in their initial disability determination. First, the examiners check to see if applicants are currently working and earning more than the substantial gainful activity (SGA) amount—$700 a month in 2000. If so, their application is denied. As can be seen in figure 3-5, almost no cases are rejected in this manner, since presumably the SSA field offices have already checked to see if applicants are working before they send applications to the disability determination office. Second, the state disability examiners determine whether the applicant has a severe impairment that is expected to last twelve months or result in death. If not, the application is denied. About 9 percent of all applicants were denied at this step in 2000. Third, the state disability examiners look to see if the impairment meets the medical listings. If the impairment is listed, applicants pass the categorical screening for disability. If the impairment is judged to be equivalent to one of the medical listings, then applicants also meet the categorical requirement for benefits. The largest share of applicants who pass the disability screening do so at this stage because their impairment either meets or equals one on the medical listing (19.5 percent of all applicants were approved at this step in 2000).

Fourth, if a decision cannot be reached on medical factors alone, applicants are evaluated in terms of residual functional capacity. If they are found to meet the demands of "past relevant work," their claim is denied (9.3 percent of all applicants were denied at this step in 2000). If individuals are deemed unable to do past relevant work, examiners determine if the impairment prevents the applicant from doing any other work. Here vocational factors are considered. If, for example, applicants' maximum sustained work capacity is limited to sedentary work and they are at least age fifty to fifty-four with less than a high school education and no skilled work experience, then they would be considered disabled and pass the categorical screening. In contrast, if applicants' previous employment experience includes skilled work, then they would not receive benefits. At this stage, 14.5 percent of all applicants were determined eligible for benefits and 12 percent were denied benefits in 2000.

Applicants who are denied benefits can ask for reconsideration. These applicants' files are then reviewed by a second team of examiners. If they are rejected after reconsideration, applicants may appeal the case to an administrative law judge (the fifth and last step in the process). At this stage, applicants will come face-to-face with a gatekeeper for the first time. Applicants denied benefits at this stage may appeal the decision to the Social Security Appeals Council and then to the District Courts. In 2000, about 40 percent of those initially denied benefits appealed the decision. About half of those who appealed the initial decision were eventually awarded benefits (SSA 2009a). For claimants who are either allowed benefits at the initial level or do not appeal, the application and decision process usually takes a few months. For those who appeal to the administrative law judge (ALJ), the process can take years.

the early 1970s because it allowed the decision-makers to give more consideration to an individual's vocational characteristics. Taking vocational factors into account means SSDI/SSI evaluators can consider an applicant's age, education level, and history of physical labor when making decisions about program eligibility. Since older, less educated, and blue-collar workers have more difficulty finding jobs once they have been unemployed than younger, better educated, and white-collar workers—regardless of impairment—the increased use of vocational factors in the determination process represents an expansion of the SSDI/SSI entry criteria. While the increased use of vocational characteristics is consistent

FIGURE 3-7

INITIAL AWARDS FOR SSDI BASED ON VOCATIONAL FACTORS, OVER TIME

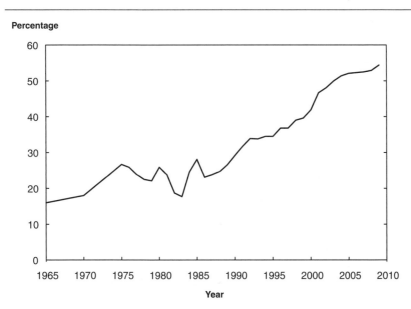

SOURCE: Data for 1975–2010 available in SSA, forthcoming. Data prior to 1975 were obtained from internal sources at the Social Security Advisory Board (SSAB) and provided by SSAB staff member Katherine Thornton.

with the positive relationship found between increases in yearly aggregate unemployment rates and SSDI acceptance rates, the increase in the use of vocational factors suggests a broader pattern of liberalization in administrative decision making.

While congressional mandates to reduce the use of these vocational criteria were not written into regulation changes, Congress communicated its displeasure to the SSA during the second half of the 1970s, and the use of these criteria decreased over 1976–1983.[13] This, in part, explains the drop in the share of beneficiaries with mental illness or musculoskeletal conditions among new enrollees over the period, but as figure 3-7 shows, the use of vocational characteristics has more than tripled since 1983. Presently, the majority of initial SSDI judgments are based on these vocational criteria rather than on the severity of an applicant's health

FIGURE 3-8
NUMBER OF ALJ HEARINGS REQUESTED OVER TIME

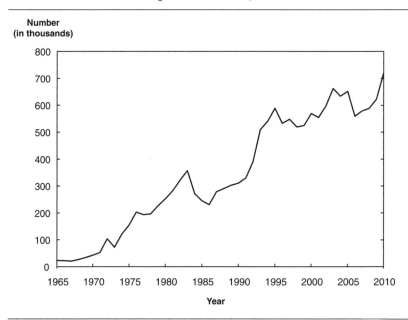

SOURCE: Data for 1975–2010 available in SSA, forthcoming. Data prior to 1975 were obtained from internal sources at the Social Security Advisory Board (SSAB) and provided by SSAB staff member Katherine Thornton.

condition alone (increasingly so in regard to mental illness and musculoskeletal conditions).

Box 3-1 discusses the five-step process for initial disability determination for SSDI and SSI-disabled adults' eligibility, but this is only the first level of evaluation these programs offer applicants. Those denied benefits initially can ask to be reconsidered. Failing reconsideration, they can appeal at the administrative law judge level. At the ALJ level, applicants can, for the first time, be represented by counsel and present expert witnesses. In contrast, the SSA can do neither at this level. A sign that the disability determination process is becoming not only more discretionary but also more time consuming is that appeals at the ALJ level have tripled since 1977 (see figure 3-8). The increased presence at ALJ hearings of

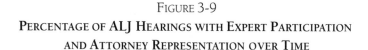

FIGURE 3-9
PERCENTAGE OF ALJ HEARINGS WITH EXPERT PARTICIPATION
AND ATTORNEY REPRESENTATION OVER TIME

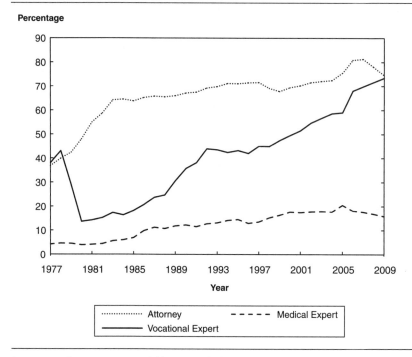

SOURCE: Data for 1997–2009 available in SSA, forthcoming. Data prior to 1975 were obtained from internal sources at the Social Security Advisory Board (SSAB) and provided by SSAB staff member Katherine Thornton.

attorneys, vocational experts, and medical experts on behalf of previously denied SSDI applicants (see figure 3-9) is another indication that decisions are becoming increasingly difficult to determine. It also suggests that the SSA's inability under current laws to bring its vocational and medical experts to these hearings has also played a part in the growth in the SSDI and SSI-disabled adult program rolls.

Summary

This chapter has shown that the growth in the disability benefit rolls is affected more by policy than by health. The program rules have directly and indirectly affected who is and is not classified as having a disability. The result of these metrics for evaluation is disability benefit rolls that far outstretch reasonable estimates of declining health in the overall population.[14] These measurements also predict substantial future program growth unless current policies are changed. The significant increase in SSDI applications in 2009 associated with the recession and the longer-term changes in the criteria for acceptance documented in this chapter portend even faster growth in the disability benefit rolls in coming years.

4

Disability Policy and
Disability Decision Making

Previous chapters have suggested a notable part of the growth in the SSDI and SSI programs is related to policy, namely the easing and more lenient implementation of program eligibility rules. Increasingly, SSDI gatekeepers are faced with the decision to accept or reject long-term unemployed workers who have serious impairments but who do not meet or exceed the medical listings for admittance to the rolls. Likewise, SSI gatekeepers increasingly are faced with the decision to accept or reject long-term welfare recipients who would not qualify on health alone. In the past, policymakers have opted to control disability program costs and caseloads by tightening the definition or application of disability standards. As discussed in chapter 3, tightening or loosening both standards and their implementation can influence caseload-to-worker ratios (see figure 3-1). As we have shown, such measures reduce disability program rolls for a while, but absent policy changes focused on reintegrating denied applicants into the labor force, such reforms cannot be sustained, resulting in the type of backlash the SSA experienced in the 1980s.

In this chapter, we suggest that a more sustainable place to begin policy reforms is well ahead of the point when individuals consider applying for SSDI or SSI benefits and long before gatekeepers are faced with the decision to place long-term unemployed workers on SSDI benefits or long-term welfare recipients on SSI benefits. It is these early actions that can more effectively increase the employment of working-age men and women with disabilities and reduce or delay their movement onto the SSDI and SSI rolls.

Disability Policy and Decision Making

The SSDI and SSI programs are intended to be last-resort income maintenance programs for those unable to perform any substantial gainful
employment activity. Applicants for both programs are screened by the SSA
to determine eligibility for disability benefits. Although SSDI and SSI use
the same disability criteria, they are very different programs with different
financing schemes. SSDI is financed through a flat-rate 1.8 percent payroll
tax split equally between employees and employers. Unlike unemployment
insurance or workers' compensation insurance, SSDI is not experience
rated, meaning all employers and employees pay the same rate regardless of
their record of SSDI program use. The tax was applied to earnings up to
$106,800 in 2010. Proceeds from these taxes are used to support payments
to SSDI beneficiaries. Revenues in excess of benefit payments are returned
to the U.S. Treasury in exchange for a bond that is saved in what is
commonly known as the Social Security Trust Fund.[1] SSI, like other
social welfare programs, is not financed from payroll or other direct taxes;
instead, it is funded with general federal tax revenue.

Both of these programs are the final part of a much larger set of public
and private programs available to individuals following the onset of a
work-limiting disability. At each point in the process, both those with a
disability and their service providers have to make decisions with respect
to their accommodation, rehabilitation, and return to work to determine
whether they should move further along the path to long-term SSDI or
SSI benefits. The SSDI and SSI systems are not passive actors in this
process. Rather, the way the SSDI and SSI systems are financed, and their
willingness to accept responsibility as the last-resort programs for those
with serious impairments who do not work, influences the way workers,
employers, and state governments respond to a worker's health shock.

As noted in previous chapters, the physical and social environment a
worker faces after the onset of a health-based impairment can be as
important as the severity of that impairment in determining whether or
how quickly the worker ends up on the long-term disability transfer rolls.
Government and private-sector institutions and programs can play a
significant role in influencing caseload growth. To illustrate this view, we
show in detail how the social environment and the actions of both the

impaired worker and his or her employer are influenced by the current SSDI system. Similarly, we show how the social environment and the actions of both the person with a disability living in a low-income household and his or her state's welfare agency are influenced by the current SSI system. We diagram how agents (employees, employers, private insurance companies, and government providers) interact and react to a worker's health shock in light of these program rules. Since the actors and paths for those moving onto SSDI are different from those considering SSI, we examine these programs separately.

SSDI: Disability Path for Those Who Have Worked

Figure 4-1a shows how workers who have a sufficient work history to be covered by SSDI make decisions after experiencing a health shock and their implications for SSDI caseloads. The decision to stay in the workforce, to seek long-term private insurance, or to apply for SSDI depends on the severity of the health shock, the impairments it causes, and the activity limitations associated with it. As previous chapters have argued, however, it also depends on the individual's social environment, including the worker's ability to receive accommodation and rehabilitation. Additionally, expected future wage earnings play a role in the decision: the greater they are, the more likely the worker is to try to continue working.[2] Just as environmental factors can encourage a focus on work following a health shock, these factors can also discourage future work. For example, workers with a higher likelihood of being accepted onto long-term private disability insurance rolls or onto the SSDI rolls will be more likely to forgo labor-market investments and apply for benefits. Similarly, the more of a worker's future wage earnings these program benefits replace, the more likely the worker is to apply for them.[3]

The duality of these incentives embedded in public insurance programs highlights the fact that social insurance has the same potential moral-hazard problem as private insurance. That is, the greater the benefits the insurance provides, the more likely the benefits will be used. Private health insurance provides a useful example—the well insured or those with low copayments are more likely to visit the doctor or use other medical services, necessary or not, than those who have higher co-pays or who have to pay for procedures out of pocket. The moral-hazard problems related to disability insurance suggest that those who are protected against loss of earnings following a health shock are less likely to work after such a shock. Although most workers who experience a limitation cannot transform themselves into candidates for SSDI benefits since the health-based criteria for eligibility are not trivial, workers with a work limitation who are having difficulty with their current jobs or who are no longer working may be influenced to apply for SSDI benefits because of the relative rewards they provide, rather than to try to remain in the labor force. For some portion of this population, the length of time they continue on the job will depend on the social institutions in place at the onset of their disability as well as their specific health or functional-limitation problems.[4]

Most studies of the behavioral consequences of disability policies have focused on how workers respond to the inevitable moral hazard

FIGURE 4-1a

DECISION TREE OF A POTENTIALLY SSDI-ELIGIBLE WORKER
REACTING TO THE ONSET OF A DISABILITY

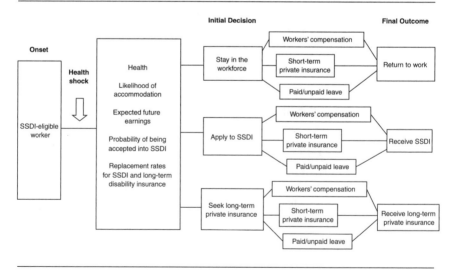

SOURCE: Authors' description of decision making following the onset of a disability.

created by social insurance, but it is also important to address how the design of social insurance affects employers' behavior. Figure 4-1b provides a useful way to think about how employers react to an employee's health shock. The figure examines how they weigh the costs and benefits of providing such a worker with accommodation or rehabilitation to delay an exit from employment or encourage a return to work versus encouraging them to move onto private disability insurance and eventually apply for SSDI benefits.

While employers' decisions will certainly depend on the health shock and its impact on the employee's ability to work, they will also consider a variety of other factors, including the costs of providing accommodation and rehabilitation relative to paying for disability transfers and finding a replacement worker. The lower the cost of accommodation and the higher the probability that it will be successful, the more likely an employer is to provide it.[5] The more the worker receiving benefits (workers' compensation,

FIGURE 4-1b

DECISION TREE OF AN EMPLOYER / INSURER REACTING
TO THE ONSET OF AN EMPLOYEE'S DISABILITY

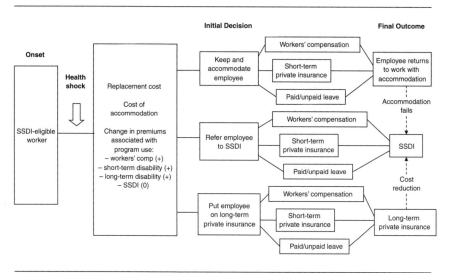

SOURCE: Authors' description of decision making following the onset of a disability.
NOTE: Change in premiums is commonly known as experience rating.

short- and long-term private insurance, and public disability) affects insurance premiums, the more likely an employer is to invest in bringing that worker back to work following a health shock. Similarly, the more expensive it is to replace the worker, the more likely an employer is to invest in returning an employee to work.

To understand how all the incentives discussed in figures 4-1a and 4-1b influence applications for SSDI, it is useful to consider the path that leads American workers with disabilities to apply for benefits. Once an impairment affects ability to work, both the workers and their employers must make important work-related decisions. For some, work is immediately impossible under any conditions, but for others, interventions can delay their movement out of the workforce. If the disability is the result of a work-related incident, then the worker and employer are subject to state workers' compensation (WC) rules that provide medical care and short- or long-term partial disability cash benefits to workers and influence employers' and employees' decisions regarding accommodation, rehabilitation, and return to work.[6]

To help manage these decisions, large employers typically use private insurance providers to evaluate their employees from the beginning of a disability's onset. Because WC is experience rated (that is, the cost of WC coverage to the firm is affected by the past record of WC benefit receipt of its employees), the additional costs of providing WC benefits to workers are initially borne by employers. Thus, they have an incentive to make decisions regarding the provision of accommodation and rehabilitation based on the full costs and benefits of maintaining or releasing the employee.[7] Likewise, because WC benefits are less than workers' wages—especially for higher wage earners—workers have an incentive to try to return to work. For workers unable to return to work after a temporary period with WC benefits, employers who provide private long-term disability insurance face the same economic incentives to maintain or release employees based on an analysis of the full costs and benefits. When employers have an incentive to consider the tradeoff between the payment of long-term disability benefits and accommodation, rehabilitation, and return to work, the incentives are better aligned to encourage workers to return to employment. Private-sector insurance providers are the agents who make these case-management decisions from the beginning.

However, because SSDI is not experience rated and employers do not directly bear the additional costs when their workers move onto the SSDI rolls, employers and their insurance agents do not have these additional costs to consider when making decisions about accommodation, rehabilitation, and return to work.[8] As a result, firms will invest less than the optimal amount in these activities and may even actively help those workers they determine eligible for private long-term disability benefits to move onto the SSDI rolls. For workers unable to perform any substantial gainful activity and who meet SSDI eligibility standards, such help is appropriate. However, when these workers could work, given an appropriate mix of accommodation and rehabilitation, these employers' actions inappropriately increase SSDI caseloads and shift the costs of long-term disability benefits from the firm and its employees to the SSDI program.

Because permanent private disability benefits and SSDI benefits are lower than workers' wage earnings, especially for higher-wage earners, workers have an incentive to try to return to work. When private insurers acting as the employer's agent provide less accommodation and rehabilitation than is appropriate and assist workers in their efforts to get onto the SSDI rolls, however, workers are more likely to focus on this path of permanent exit from employment than to try to return to work.

When a disability is not job related, short-term cash benefits funded by mandatory employee contributions are available in only five states. Nevertheless, most firms provide their employees with sick days and vacation days that may initially offset lost wages due to a disability. Far fewer employees are provided with the opportunity to obtain long-term disability insurance within their firms' compensation packages. Firms that do offer such benefits have similar incentives to reduce costs, as discussed previously. However, because SSDI is not experience rated, these firms and their workers are likely to underinvest in accommodation and rehabilitation and put additional pressure on the SSDI program.

The only option for long-term disability cash transfers for workers whose employers do not provide private disability insurance, unless they have purchased long-term disability insurance on their own, is SSDI. Once they have used up their sick days and vacation days, such workers must return to work. Those who do not and are dismissed from their jobs may be eligible for unemployment benefits, but these benefits are temporary. Even for these workers, it may be in a firm's interest to provide some accommodation, however, since replacing them will result in additional hiring and training costs, especially if the employee with a disability has special skills specific to the firm. This may also be the case if poor treatment by the firm would affect workplace morale and the firm's reputation. Additionally, the ADA requires firms to provide reasonable accommodation for workers with disabilities.[9]

Again, because SSDI is financed by a flat-rate payroll tax rather than experience rated, employers do not face any of the added costs of moving workers to the SSDI program, and no agent will be assigned to manage disabled workers' cases in a way that provides the appropriate mix of accommodation and rehabilitation relative to long-term disability transfers. In such circumstances, it is primarily left to the worker to decide whether to pursue employment or focus on getting into the SSDI program.

Many workers who experience a health shock on the job that limits their ability to work are able to continue on the job. For some, SSDI may eventually be inevitable, but their movement onto the rolls can be delayed depending on the social institutions they face. In addition to their health condition, workers will also consider how likely they are to be accepted for SSDI benefits if they apply, known as the SSDI allowance rate; the level of benefits they will receive if eligible, known as the SSDI replacement rate; their future labor earnings if they continue to try to remain in the labor force; and their likelihood of receiving accommodation. The amount of accommodation they will receive will depend on the costs employers bear for providing it relative to the costs they are likely to incur for an increase in experience-rated premiums they must pay for workers' compensation, short- and long-term private disability insurance, and SSDI.

SSI-Disabled Adults: Disability Path for Those with Limited Work Histories

Figures 4-2a and 4-2b provide analogous decision trees for potential candidates for the SSI-disabled adults program and for the state agencies with which they interact. While the SSDI and SSI-disabled adults programs share the same medical standards for eligibility, they focus on very different populations. SSDI primarily provides insurance against lost earnings for workers with an established work history, and its monthly benefits (primary insurance amount [PIA]) are progressive so they replace a larger share of the average indexed monthly earnings (AIME) of lower-wage workers. The maximum benefits most workers who meet the medical test and the earnings-history test for SSDI benefits could receive from the SSI-disabled adults program would be well below their SSDI benefit. For example, as seen in figure 4-3—which traces the relationship between AIME and PIA—the monthly federal SSI benefit in 2010 was $674 (this is also known as the federal benefit rate [FBR]). A worker with an AIME of $749 ($8,988 per year) would receive an SSDI benefit of this value. A minimum-wage worker earning $7.25 per hour would have to work only 1,240 hours per year (less than 25 hours per week) to generate an AIME that exceeded the federal SSI benefit.[10]

As such, most working-age people who are potential candidates for the SSI-disabled adults program have little or no work history, either because

FIGURE 4-2a
DECISION TREE OF AN SSI-ELIGIBLE PERSON
REACTING TO THE ONSET OF A DISABILITY

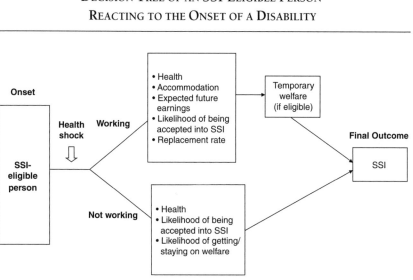

SOURCE: Authors' description of the decision making process following the onset of a disability.

they are young or because they are older but have a weak educational background and few marketable job skills. Thus, a work limitation is often only one of the factors preventing those considered eligible for the SSI-disabled adults program, but not for SSDI benefits, from working. It is likely their lack of job skills would make their potential wages low and their unemployment rates high even if costless accommodation were provided to offset their disabilities. Fewer than 30 percent of SSI-disabled adults beneficiaries were working at the time of the onset of their disability (Bound, Burkhauser, and Nichols 2003). For them, the issue is more about how they can manage some minimum level of economic status, given weak job-market skills.

Those who are working face the same employment-related issues discussed for those eligible for SSDI benefits (see the work path route in figure 4-1a), but they are more likely to be employed by a firm without private disability insurance; they are less likely to be candidates their

FIGURE 4-2b

DECISION TREE OF A STATE GOVERNMENT REACTING TO THE ONSET OF A DISABILITY OF A LOW-INCOME ADULT WHO MAY BE ELIGIBLE FOR SSI BENEFITS

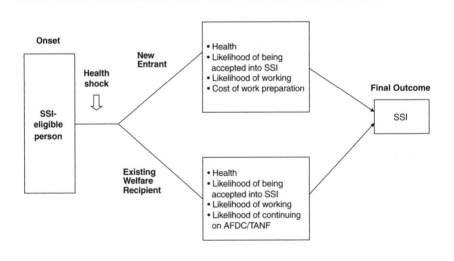

SOURCE: Authors' description of the decision making process following the onset of a disability.

FIGURE 4-3

SSDI AND SSI BENEFITS BY EARNINGS LEVEL FOR A SINGLE, DISABLED INDIVIDUAL
LIVING INDEPENDENTLY WITH ZERO EARNINGS AND ASSETS BELOW THE SSI LIMIT

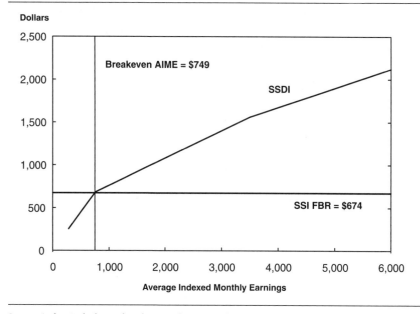

SOURCE: Authors' calculations based on Social Security Administration data.

employer would consider for accommodation and rehabilitation, since, on average, they have shorter work histories with their firms and are less costly to replace. They are also less likely to have overall work histories that make them eligible for SSDI benefit consideration. Like SSDI-covered workers, they weigh the advantages of a continued struggle in the labor market relative to, in their case, application for SSI-disabled adults benefits. Since SSI benefits also offer immediate access to Medicaid, movement onto the rolls can be an attractive path for some of these workers.[11]

The majority of SSI-disabled adults program applicants do not have a tie to an employer, however. Over 50 percent are already receiving means-tested government transfer program benefits at the time they apply for SSI-disabled adults benefits. They also do not have a strong private network of income security. Only 33 percent are married, and fewer than 20 percent of applicants report that their spouses have labor earnings (Bound, Burkhauser, and Nichols 2003). For these individuals, the decision to apply for SSI-disabled adults benefits is affected by the severity of their health shock along with environmental factors, such as the probability of getting or continuing to receive welfare benefits, the probability of getting onto SSI, and the value of SSI benefits relative to the income available from the network of welfare benefits, family support, and potential future earnings (see the nonwork path in figure 4-2b).

In many respects, this working-age, mostly single, lower-skilled, and low-income population more closely resembles the U.S. welfare population than it does the insured working-age population eligible for SSDI (Daly 1998). The similarities between the SSI-disabled adults population and the general welfare population make it important to consider the potential interactions between the two programs (AFDC/TANF and SSI). This is true for both individuals and state administrators. As in the case of SSDI, disincentives to provide rehabilitation for return to work again arise, but now they do so with respect to state behavior rather than firm behavior (see figure 4-2b). The potential for overuse of a benefit program intended to be a path of last resort is common to both programs.[12] To see how welfare reform can affect SSI-disabled adults program applications, it is useful to think again about how TANF works.[13] A major feature of welfare reform was the devolution of federal funds to the states via block grants with relatively few mandates on their use, provided they targeted poor families. In establishing the size of these block grants, the federal government committed to provide states the same nominal level of welfare funding they were receiving in 1996 even if TANF expenses fell, which happened. The states used part of these extra funds for work-based programs targeted at single mothers, but they may also use them for more general state programs targeted at low-income populations. In this way, it is in the state's interest to focus more resources on work-based programs.

As a consequence of this funding arrangement, states have an incentive to move their most difficult-to-employ working-age population to federally supported programs. In the case of the welfare population, the federal program is the SSI-disabled adults program. Although this is not an option for everyone, the combination of health and vocational criteria embedded in the SSI eligibility standards indicates the potential that some fraction of the hard-to-employ welfare population will become eligible for SSI.[14] Since states are not experience rated based on the number of the poor they help onto SSI—like employers who do not incur any of the marginal costs of moving their workers onto SSDI—states provide less rehabilitation and training for working-age people with disabilities who live in poor households than they would if they were fully responsible for the costs associated with the long-term, last-resort SSI payments to this nonworking population.

Summary

In this chapter we have shown how current SSDI and SSI program rules leave the federal government responsible for a great share of the costs associated with providing long-term disability transfers for working-age people with disabilities who do not work. Because employers have no liability for SSDI program benefits paid to former employees, employers do not have an incentive to accommodate and rehabilitate employees who could otherwise receive SSDI benefits. Similar incentives lead state governments to move individuals to the federally funded SSI-disabled adults programs. Unlike the prowork incentives inherent in welfare as reformed, antiwork incentives in SSDI/SSI have led to a disability system designed to enroll too many individuals for long-term cash benefits in lieu of work. Both the SSDI and SSI-disabled adults programs have failed to signal the true costs of benefits, which has resulted in a higher number of enrollees because either employers or state governments did not provide the accommodation, rehabilitation, and training needed. These same beneficiaries may have received this assistance if employers and states were held more directly responsible for SSDI and SSI costs. The outcomes of the current system were shown in previous chapters: rapid growth in program costs (see figure I-1) and caseloads (see figure 1-1) that threaten the long-term stability of the SSDI and SSI programs, along with declining employment rates (see figure 1-4) and stagnant economic status (see figure 1-3) of the working-age population with disabilities they serve.

5

Lessons from Dutch
Disability Policy Reforms

In 2002, the Netherlands initiated reforms to its national disability system that significantly reduced disability cash-transfer rolls while maintaining a strong, albeit less generous, social minimum safety net for those who do not work. These reforms were prompted by many of the same pressures currently burdening the U.S. system, including rapid and unsustainable caseload growth and burgeoning costs. Previous attempts to reform the system by lowering benefit levels and tightening eligibility rules reduced the program population but not sufficiently to solve the long-run problems of expensive and rising rolls. The 2002 reforms were much more fundamental and based on the recognition that disability program rules, the administration of those rules, and the methods established to pay for these programs greatly influenced the behavior of key actors—employees and employers—at the time a worker experienced the onset of a disability. By recognizing that the previous system did little to signal the true cost—to either workers or their employers—of moving onto the long-term disability transfer rolls, Dutch policymakers were able to restructure the program so both employers and employees more directly observed and bore the expense. These changes have had a significant impact; since the reforms, the Netherlands has seen a different mix of accommodation, rehabilitation, and cash transfers, and its disability caseload is no longer growing at an unsustainable pace. Here we review disability program growth in the Netherlands, link it to changes in the country's disability policies, show that, while

This chapter is an extension of Burkhauser, Daly, and de Jong (2008). It was completed with the impeccable guidance of Philip de Jong.

difficult to achieve, disability policy reform is possible, and draw lessons from the Dutch experience for fundamental reform of the U.S. SSDI program.

Disability Caseloads

Figure 5-1 compares caseload growth in SSDI and SSI for the United States with caseload growth in the Netherlands. The numbers for the United

FIGURE 5-1
U.S. SSDI AND SSI-DISABLED BENEFICIARIES AND
DUTCH DISABILITY BENEFICIARIES PER THOUSAND WORKERS
AGES FIFTEEN TO SIXTY-FOUR OVER TIME

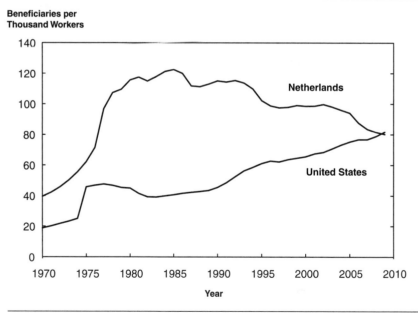

SOURCE: Authors' updated figure from Aarts, Burkhauser, and de Jong (1998); updated data from three sources: Centraal Planbureau [Central Planning Bureau] (1998–2010); Uitvoering Werknemersverzekeringen [National Social Insurance Institute] (n.d.); Social Security Administration, various years a; and International Labour Organization (1998–2010).
NOTE: The U.S. data cover all workers ages fifteen to sixty-four. The Dutch data are for workers ages fifteen to sixty-four, adjusted for hours differences between part- and full-time workers. Separate analysis not shown here shows that these results are not dependent on the definitional differences.

States are the same as those reported in figure 3-1. The figure reports the levels and trends in the number of working-age people receiving disability transfer benefits per thousand economically active persons for the United States and the Netherlands. Because a country's workers ultimately provide the resources made available through government disability transfers, this is a useful measure of the relative burden the disability transfer population places on the working population in a given country. While it is only one means of approximating the importance of disability policies across countries, it nonetheless captures the differences policies make in the levels and trends in a country's caseload-per-worker ratio over time. Underlying this comparison is the notion that differences over time in caseloads across countries are more likely to be related to differences in policies than to differences in health.

Both the Netherlands and the United States caseload-per-worker ratios have grown substantially since 1970. While increases to the U.S. ratio occurred primarily in the 1970s with a relatively level period in the 1980s and then relatively rapid growth thereafter, in the Netherlands growth was extremely rapid in the 1970s and early 1980s before coming down in steps in 1987, 1994, and 2002. As figure 5-1 illustrates, due to the reforms over the 2002–2006 period in the Netherlands, together with the continuing rise in U.S. caseloads per worker since the 1980s, the Netherlands' program levels dropped below those of the United States in 2009.

A brief history of Dutch disability policy changes shows how important they have been in affecting the size of the Dutch disability transfer population and offers some clues as to how U.S. policy might be changed.

Path to Disability Benefits in the Netherlands

As in the United States, the disability system in the Netherlands contains both a social insurance program that protects workers against lost labor earnings and a program that provides a social minimum for disabled adults with little or no work history. A separate social minimum scheme for the disabled self-employed ended in 2004. The Dutch social insurance program (WAO/WIA) provides cash transfers to working-age men and women based on lost labor earnings. The Netherlands does not have a separate program similar to workers' compensation. Rather, it has a longer-term disability transfer program that, together with the sickness benefits all private firms must offer their workers, provides a comprehensive system of both partial and total disability benefits to workers regardless of how or where their disability occurred. The Dutch also have a categorical disability-based welfare program (Wajong) that, unlike the general welfare scheme, is not means tested. This program is similar to the SSI-disabled adults program in that it targets men and women whose disabilities occurred prior to their entrance into the labor force and are severe enough that they have not engaged in full-time employment as adults. Figure 5-2 traces the ups and downs in both Dutch social insurance and welfare disability caseloads between 1970 and 2009. As the figure shows, in the 1970s, Dutch disability insurance caseloads as a share of the country's entire population grew rapidly and their disability system was universally considered out of control.

One reason for this rapid growth was the relatively generous benefits that the system provided. As noted earlier, the first level of protection for Dutch workers was a universal sickness benefit—essentially a universal short-term disability system. In the 1970s, government payments from this program replaced up to 80 percent of net-of-tax wage earnings for up to one year. However, most employees (90 percent) and all civil servants had the rest of their net-of-tax earnings replaced by collective-bargaining agreements with their employers. These replacement rates were far in excess of comparable programs in the United States. Sickness benefits were payable for up to twelve months. After one year, employees still receiving benefits were eligible for disability benefit screening. Workers with chronic conditions that caused a reduction in their capacity to perform work commensurate with their job training and work history were eligible for disability benefits. Those judged fully disabled were eligible for benefits equal to 80 percent of their previous before-tax earnings. Those judged partially disabled (those with some residual earnings capacity) were eligible for partial benefits; the minimum degree of impairment for eligibility was 15 percent.

A critical challenge in this system was how to determine the level of residual earnings capacity. Although efforts were made to judge which

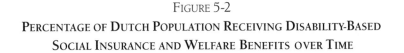

FIGURE 5-2
PERCENTAGE OF DUTCH POPULATION RECEIVING DISABILITY-BASED
SOCIAL INSURANCE AND WELFARE BENEFITS OVER TIME

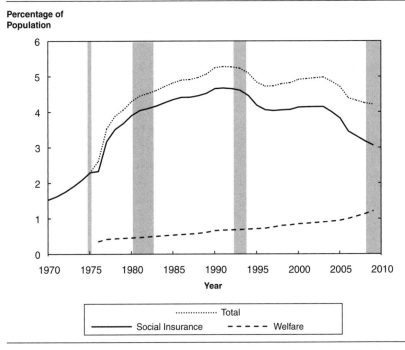

SOURCE: Authors' updated figure from Aarts, Burkhauser, and de Jong (1998); updated data from three sources: Centraal Planbureau [Central Planning Bureau] (1998–2000); Uitvoering Werknemersverzekeringen [National Social Insurance Institute] (n.d.); Social Security Administration, various years a; and International Labour Organization (1998–2010).
NOTE: Gray bars denote official recession dating.

jobs were commensurate with the worker's current health-impaired job skills and how those jobs compared to previous employment, in many cases these estimates diverged from actual earnings, especially when the worker remained unemployed. In such cases, it was difficult to disentangle the lack of earnings or employment caused by the reduction in the worker's job skills due to the health impairment from that caused by general market conditions, discrimination, or unwillingness to work. Dutch policymakers resolved this difficulty with an article in the country's Disability Insurance Act that required "labor-market consideration" to be part of the final determination of residual earnings capacity to establish partial benefits. Under this article, unless disability evaluators could prove otherwise, they were required to attribute a partially disabled worker's lack of employment to discriminatory behavior. The result was that it became "administrative practice" to treat unemployed, partially disabled persons as if they were fully disabled. That interpretation of the law made assessing lost earnings capacity unnecessary beyond the minimum 15 percent, since that became sufficient to entitle a person to full benefits. This essentially made the Dutch partial disability system a very generous full disability program.

The relative generosity of the Dutch system during this period was further increased by the exclusion of disability benefits from social security taxes. Dutch social security taxes increased substantially in the 1970s, and the burden was borne entirely by workers not on disability benefits. The differential treatment of wages and disability benefits resulted in a relative gain in income for those on the disability system; while the average real after-tax wages of workers rose by about 7 percent, the average disability benefit grew by 16 percent over the decade. These increases in eligibility and in the generosity of the system had a profound effect on the size of the disability transfer population per thousand workers. It nearly tripled over the decade from around forty per thousand workers in 1970 to around one hundred and fifteen per thousand in 1980, as figure 5-1 shows.

The serious recession of the early 1980s and the growing costs of the disability system put pressure on the Dutch government to reduce the growth of disability transfers. Reforms initiated between 1982 and 1987 were the first of three major efforts over the next two decades to regain control of the Dutch disability transfer system. By 1985, a series of cuts in the replacement rate had effectively lowered it from 80 percent of before-tax income to 70 percent of after-tax income for both new entrants and current beneficiaries. The cumulative effect of those cuts was a reduction of almost 25 percent in the net real transfer income of disabled workers over the first five years of the decade, relative to a drop of 10 percent in the real net earnings of workers who remained in the workforce. For the median worker, after-tax replacement rates dropped from 87 percent at the end of the 1970s to 70 percent at the end of the 1980s, but that did not halt system growth completely and, after sustained public debate, the

Dutch parliament passed additional disability amendments that took effect in 1987.[1] The most important was the abolition of the labor market consideration rule. As shown in figure 5-1, while these reforms reduced the ratio somewhat over this period, there were still more than one hundred caseloads per thousand workers in 1987, which was much higher than the ratio at the start of the 1970s and much higher than the approximately forty caseloads per thousand workers in the United States.

Despite the legal ban on including labor-market considerations in their assessments, disability adjudicators still tended either to grant or deny full benefits. Denial rates remained quite low, suggesting that the legal change did not stop the de facto use of labor-market considerations in the adjudication process. After 1988, the caseload-per-worker ratio grew again, and it continued growing through the early 1990s, when the Dutch adopted another set of reforms.[2]

The 1994 reforms included further tightening of eligibility criteria. The concept of "commensurate" employment was broadened to include all generally accepted jobs that are compatible with one's residual capacities, irrespective of former vocational status, work history, and education. In addition, the reforms required that the causal relationship between impairment and ability to work be more objectively assessable. Finally, disability benefit status was limited to a maximum of five years, at which point a beneficiary would have to be reassessed. Benefit levels were also cut after a certain period on the program depending on one's age at the onset of disability. The most provocative reform was the implementation of a review of the disability status of current beneficiaries under age forty-five based on the new and more stringent eligibility criteria.

Additionally, for the first time, firms were made responsible for an employee's first six weeks of sick pay. The introduction of this type of privatization of the disability system was unprecedented in the Netherlands, and it was the first serious attempt by Dutch disability policy to encourage firms to provide for their employees more accommodation, rehabilitation, and options to return to work as an alternative to simply pushing them onto the disability transfer rolls. The mandate for firms to bear the full responsibility for sick pay was extended from six weeks to one year in 1996. Figure 5-1 shows that as a result of these reforms, most especially the reviews of current beneficiaries, the ratio of disability caseloads per worker dropped slightly below one hundred for the first time since 1977. The decline in this ratio stopped, however, and by 2002, it had once again climbed to almost one hundred beneficiaries per thousand workers.[3] Over this period, the Organisation for Economic Co-operation and Development (OECD) still ranked the Netherlands among its member states with the highest disability beneficiary population rate per worker (OECD 2003).

In 2002, the Dutch disability system began to phase in the third and most significant set of reforms. These reforms culminated in the establishment of a new disability insurance scheme in 2004—WIA—which completely replaced the WAO scheme that had been in place since 1967.[4] To paraphrase President Bill Clinton's words with respect to U.S. welfare reform, these systemic reforms changed disability policy as they knew it in the Netherlands. At their heart were changes that increased the incentives of both employees and their employers to invest more time and effort in accommodation and rehabilitation following the onset of a disability.

Foremost among the reforms was the extension from one year to two years of the mandate that firms (including small employers) bear full responsibility for employees' sick pay.[5] A reduction in the maximum benefit from 100 to 85 percent of gross wages eased slightly the financial burden the additional year of sickness pay put on firms. These changes effectively meant that during the first two years following a health shock, workers were the responsibility of the firm and not eligible for long-term government-provided disability benefits. During these two years, employers are required to allow workers receiving sickness benefits to continue with the firm. Employers can only dismiss employees who refuse to cooperate in a reasonable work-resumption plan. Under the reforms, firms also have a set of prescribed rehabilitation and accommodation activities that they (via a private occupational health agency) must provide to try either to retain disabled employees or to find alternative employment for them during those two years. Every firm is mandated to contract a prescribed set of occupational health services, such as medical experts, to check the legitimacy of absences. These rules for sick employees and their employers are laid down in an act called the Gatekeeper Protocol.

When the two years are complete and workers are allowed to apply for long-term disability benefits, they are required to provide documentation regarding return-to-work efforts during the two-year period. Disability insurance benefit claims are admissible only if they are accompanied by a report containing an assessment as to why the plan has not resulted in work resumption. The claim is not processed by the National Social Insurance Institute (NSII)—the public organization responsible for adjudicating disability benefit claims—if the report is delayed or incomplete or if it is clear that the rehabilitation efforts were insufficient. Depending on the seriousness of the negligence, the caseworker at the NSII can return the reintegration report and give the employer the opportunity to complete it, or the caseworker can start a sanction procedure against the employer. In 2007, nearly 14 percent of disability insurance claims were returned to employers and the employer continued to be responsible for employing the worker until the claim was processed or the worker had returned to his old or a new job.

Reforms at the front end of the process were accompanied by significant reforms in the longer-term benefit program. These reforms split the previous all-encompassing disability benefits scheme into two separate programs. The first provides benefits to those judged to have an unrecoverable loss of earnings capacity of at least 80 percent. These individuals are eligible for full and permanent disability benefits replacing 75 percent of gross earnings (with a cap on covered earnings of $49,300 per year in 2011). The second provides benefits to those judged to have a loss of earnings capacity between 35 and 80 percent and to those who are fully disabled when their claim is examined but are expected to recover (part of) their earning capacity. These individuals are eligible for partial benefits and temporary full benefits. Partial beneficiaries can receive up to 70 percent of gross earnings, but the percentage varies depending on actual work behavior, and significant incentives have been built into the program to encourage beneficiaries to work to their estimated earnings capacity. Those who were on the disability rolls and under age forty-five at the time these reforms were made were reevaluated based on the new, stricter eligibility rules. Now, for example, a 100 percent loss of earnings capacity is limited to those who are institutionalized or incapable of performing regular activities of daily living independently.[6]

Under the reforms, all employers pay for the full and permanent disability program through a uniform pay-as-you-go premium rate. Employers also pay to fund the publicly run partial disability program, but they can opt out of it by enrolling their workers with a private insurer instead. Either way, employers now pay experience-rated premiums that cover the first ten years of partial disability benefit receipt. After ten years, benefits are covered by the uniform pay-as-you-go rates that also cover the fully and permanently disabled and the stock of current beneficiaries under the old system. The current Dutch government has put full privatization of the partial benefit program on its agenda. If this plan is approved, all Dutch employers, irrespective of their size, will be responsible for benefit payment over a maximum of twelve years (two years sickness and ten years partial disability benefits). This long risk period increases the potential gains by firms of providing effective accommodation and rehabilitation.

Based on these reforms, the Dutch disability system, long seen as out of control, is now considered by Prinz and Tompson (2009) in their comparison of OECD disability systems as one that has learned from its mistakes and provides an example for other OECD countries to follow. While it is still too early to determine the full effect of these policy changes on the Dutch disability beneficiary population, Van Sonsbeek (2010) provides the first microsimulation of the consequences of the post-2002 round of policy changes discussed above. He estimates that the combined impact of the introduction of experience rating together with the introduction of the statutory Gatekeeper Protocol and stricter examinations will reduce the projected long-term number of disability beneficiaries by 600,000 and that the introduction of the new WIA scheme will further reduce that projected number by 250,000 by 2040, as compared to a "no-change scenario."

As shown in figure 5-1, the increased integration of the new disability system—which forces employers to choose between the costs of disability transfers and workplace accommodation and rehabilitation more carefully, and which reduces the accessibility and generosity of disability insurance for employees—has already resulted in a decline in the case-load-per-worker ratio in the Netherlands since 2002. In 2009, the Netherlands had eighty caseloads per thousand workers, the lowest the ratio had been since 1976. In contrast, the United States ratio, which has been rising steadily since the early 1990s, continued to do so over this period and stood at eighty-two caseloads per thousand workers in 2009.

As a result, the Dutch ratio, which in 1985 was three times that of the United States—one hundred and twenty versus forty—dipped below that of the United States in 2009, for the first time.

This decline in overall Dutch disability caseloads is especially striking, given that it includes rapid growth in the categorical disability welfare population (Wajong), shown in figure 5-2. The Wajong program provides a flat benefit at the social minimum level, financed from general revenue. Unlike the more general social minimum welfare program, it is not means tested. Eligible youth are entitled to benefits beginning at age eighteen. The number of beneficiaries in this program, which began in 1976, has steadily increased to 1.1 percent of the entire population (1.6 percent of the adult population, ages fifteen to sixty-four, not shown) or approximately 179,000 beneficiaries at the end of 2009. This compares to 2.3 percent of the United States adult population receiving SSI-disabled adult benefits in 2009 (figure 1-1). Almost all Wajong beneficiaries are considered fully disabled, not because they have no earnings capacity, but because their earnings capacity is lower than the relatively high minimum hourly wage in the Netherlands. Hence, while they may be fully capable of doing productive work in the labor market, employers do not hire them because all employees must be paid the statutory minimum wage. At current inflow rates, Van Sonsbeek (2010) estimates an increase in this program of 200,000 beneficiaries by 2040, which will offset part of the decline in the growth of beneficiaries discussed above.

The growth in the Wajong program reflects a general trend toward diagnosing behavioral difficulties in children as medical disorders. Dutch programs offering provisions for children and youth with functional limitations, like special schools, supplemental child-care benefits, and mental health care for young adults, are surging. However, the growth is limited to certain diagnostic groups: psychiatric and neurological disorders such as autism, attention deficit hyperactivity disorder (ADHD), pervasive development disorder not otherwise specified (PDD-NOS), and learning difficulties. Medical specialists and gatekeepers of these programs find it difficult to assess the work and learning capacities of these young people accurately and to counsel them toward appropriate paid employment. Because they have little guidance on how to enter the workforce, and because no special programs exist to allow them to work for wage rates below the minimum, the vast majority of such children are likely to end up in the Wajong program rather than using their productive capacities in the labor force (Suijker 2007).

Given the trend results pictured in figures 5-1 and 5-2, it is clear the social insurance reforms of 2002 are responsible for the declines seen in the disability transfer population since their implementation. Less clear is whether working-age men and women with disabilities moved to other government transfer programs or into work following the reforms. The Netherlands does not have an equivalent to the U.S. Current Population Survey that

FIGURE 5-3

PERCENTAGE OF DUTCH POPULATION ENROLLED IN
CASH-TRANSFER PROGRAMS OVER TIME

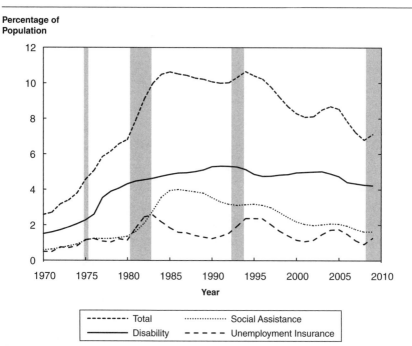

SOURCE: Authors' updated figure from Aarts, Burkhauser, and de Jong (1998); updated data from three sources: Centraal Planbureau [Central Planning Bureau] (1998–2010); Uitvoering Werknemersverzekeringen [National Social Insurance Institute] (n.d.); Social Security Administration, various years a; and International Labour Organization (1998–2010).
NOTE: Gray bars denote official recession dating.

would allow us to track the employment and economic well-being of the working-age population with and without disabilities before and after this policy change. However, figure 5-3 provides some evidence that this disability policy change did not simply shift people from the disability rolls to unemployment or general welfare rolls.

Figure 5-3 tracks caseloads for the major Dutch cash-transfer programs for working-age people who do not work—the disability, unemployment insurance, and social assistance programs—from 1970 to 2009 as a share of the total Dutch population. We have already discussed the rapid rise in the disability caseload that began in the 1970s, reached a peak in the mid-1980s, and, after several attempts at reform, now appears under control. Figure 5-3 shows that social assistance caseloads also peaked in 1986 and, with some fluctuations based on the business cycle, have been declining ever since. The same is true with respect to the unemployment insurance caseload since 1995. However, in this case, business-cycle fluctuations are even more pronounced. Figure 5-3 shows that caseloads for all three programs have fallen since 2004. The conclusion, therefore, is that there is little evidence that the Dutch disability population has simply moved from the disability program to general social assistance or unemployment insurance.

This conclusion is reinforced by the trend depicted in figure 5-4, which shows that the Dutch welfare state grew over the 1970–1980 period. The recession of the early 1980s induced a surge in both unemployment and social assistance benefits and a decrease in employment rates. Since 1985, in addition to disability reforms, reforms in social assistance and unemployment insurance have led to a fall in the ratio of caseloads per thousand workers from over 260 in 1985 to approximately 130 in 2008, the lowest point for this ratio since 1975. The recession of 2009 has increased this ratio slightly but not nearly as much as during the early years of the 1980s.

A recently concluded longitudinal study of a cohort of 4,000 employees who were still on the sickness rolls after nine months provides another piece of evidence that such workers, who under the old system would have been likely to go from the sickness rolls onto the long-term disability rolls, are not simply moving onto a different transfer program. After 27 months following their first receipt of sickness benefits, 52 percent were fully back to work and another 18 percent had partially resumed their

FIGURE 5-4
TOTAL DUTCH CASH-TRANSFER CASELOADS
PER THOUSAND WORKERS OVER TIME

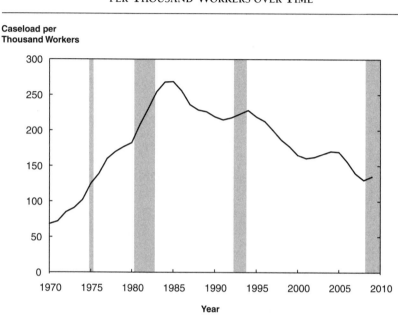

SOURCE: Authors' updated figure from Aarts, Burkhauser, and de Jong (1998); updated data from three sources: Centraal Planbureau [Central Planning Bureau] (1998–2010); Uitvoering Werknemersverzekeringen [National Social Insurance Institute] (n.d.); Social Security Administration, various years a; and International Labour Organization (1998–2010).
NOTE: Gray bars denote official recession dating.

work. Another 26 percent applied for long-term disability benefit, and two-thirds of these claimants were admitted to the disability benefit rolls. Hence, the disability benefit entry rate in this cohort of long-term (nine months) sickness beneficiaries was only 18 percent (see Everhardt and de Jong forthcoming).

Lessons for Reforming U.S. Disability Policy

The 2002 Dutch disability policy reforms and their effects on disability outcomes suggest that systemic reform of the U.S. SSDI program is possible and plausibly beneficial. A decade ago, Dutch policymakers faced many of the same pressures currently challenging the U.S. disability insurance system: rapid growth in the rolls, unsustainable growth in expenditures, and a mix of incentives that produced these outcomes. Like the United States, the Dutch had a long history of trying to reform their disability program on the margins, by lowering benefit levels and tightening eligibility rules. A key lesson that comes from their experience is that while such reforms will lead to short-run reductions in program populations, such changes do not permanently solve more fundamental policy design flaws.

The 2002 Dutch reforms were more structural. By requiring both employers and employees to bear the costs of the disability program more directly, the 2002 reforms altered the incentives workers and their employers face. Making employers responsible for the first two years of short-term disability benefit payments and a much longer period of partial disability payments, as well as requiring workers to enter into employer-provided rehabilitation programs, better signaled the true cost of moving individuals with disabilities onto long-term cash-transfer rolls. In doing so, it increased the amount of accommodation and rehabilitation provided to workers following a health shock, and it slowed their movement onto the long-term disability transfer rolls. The agents chosen by employers to manage these decisions were private-sector insurance firms that now provide the case-management necessary to make effective decisions with respect to accommodation and rehabilitation immediately following the onset of disability.

More than in the past, the 2002 Dutch reforms focused on slowing down long-term disability program growth at the entry point. Although this early intervention model is well known among gatekeepers in the private disability insurance system, it is less often part of a national program and, we argue, must be at the heart of all serious efforts to stem the tide of new beneficiaries to the SSDI program.

While the United States is unlikely to adopt mandates like those requiring Dutch employers to take full responsibility for their employees' first two years of short-term disability payments, we argue that it is important for firms and workers to more clearly recognize the additional burden their choices place on the SSDI system.[7] Because U.S. employers incur no additional costs when their workers move onto the SSDI rolls—

SSDI benefits are financed by a flat-rate 1.8 percent payroll tax—they do not recognize the real costs incurred when they fail to provide accommodation, rehabilitation, and return-to-work efforts. Similarly, employers who do provide safe workplaces or accommodation to their workers following the onset of a disability receive no direct cost offset for this behavior in regard to SSDI taxes.

One way to make employers recognize these added costs is to use experience rating to determine SSDI employer taxes: raise the tax on firms whose workers enroll in the system at above-average rates and lower the SSDI taxes on firms whose workers enroll at below-average rates. This is the system used to fund state unemployment insurance and WC benefits, and it could be implemented for disability benefits as well. Such a reform, which we will discuss more fully in chapter 7, would much more clearly signal the true cost of moving individuals with disabilities onto long-term cash-transfer rolls and make employers more likely to provide greater accommodation and rehabilitation to their workers immediately following the onset of a disability. This is the same type of structural change that underlies the 2002 Dutch disability policy reforms.[8]

Summary

Disability policy in the Netherlands in the 1970s offered access to full and permanent disability benefits that made it possible for those with as little as a 15 percent loss in earnings capacity to receive benefits close to their net-of-taxes labor earnings. The generosity of this system led to unsustainable growth in benefit rolls and costs, ultimately forcing Dutch policymakers to fundamentally change the system. The 2002 disability reforms produced a much more integrated disability system in which initial decisions with respect to accommodation, rehabilitation, and return to work are almost entirely handled by the private sector and in which long-term disability benefits become available from the government only after two years of employer-funded sick leave.

This brief history of Dutch disability policy shows that while Dutch workers' movements onto the long-term disability transfer programs were affected by the onset of a work limitation, they were also influenced by the policy environment the workers faced. Paramount among these policy variables was the disability program rules that provided incongruent incentives to continue working or apply for disability benefits. Likewise, the decisions employers made in response to the onset of their workers' limitations were influenced by disability program rules. Changing those signals so that both employers and employees bore the costs of the disability program more directly resulted in a more appropriate mix of accommodation and rehabilitation.

6

Disability Policy for Children

The SSI-disabled children population is small compared to the other U.S. cash-transfer programs targeted at individuals with disabilities. As such, it is generally overlooked during discussions of disability policy reform. Recent growth in the program, combined with the fact that so many SSI-disabled children program beneficiaries move directly onto the SSI-disabled adult rolls, however, makes the SSI-disabled children program worth examining.

The program is complicated. Unlike the programs for adults with disabilities, SSI-disabled children benefits flow to the families of children with disabilities, rather than to the children themselves. On one hand, this seems sensible since these families are responsible for the care of the child. On the other hand, the provision of cash support to low-income families who have a disabled child raises the same issues discussed for the SSDI and SSI-disabled adults programs: namely, problems of moral hazard and unintended incentives that create the potential for the program to expand beyond its original target population and goals.

Data on SSI-disabled children caseloads suggest that this potential expansion may have become a reality. The SSI-disabled children program has grown substantially over time and in a way that seems at odds with data on child health and disability. This growth raises the concern that the program is increasingly being used as a general long-term support program for children in low-income families. While the outcome of these transfers (more support to low-income children) may be socially desirable, delivering such protection through the disability system is likely inefficient. Moreover, such transfers may not be equitable, since only a subset of low-income families has a child who qualifies for the disability benefit.[1] Finally, if, as the data indicate, entry into the SSI-disabled children program likely means enrolling in the SSI-disabled adults programs once of age, the current formulation of the program may be detrimental to the long-term development of the children it targets. To the extent that a different program design might have provided these children with employment-oriented investments to enable them to enter the workforce as adults, the current SSI-disabled children program may be permanently limiting the economic status of its beneficiaries.

Original Rationale and Program Evolution

The SSI-disabled children program provides cash benefits to families with low income and a disabled child. The program does not provide services to children with disabilities, nor does it tie benefits to the purchase of services for the disabled child.[2] The program began in 1973, and its design reflects the composition of potential recipients at that time. In the 1970s, the typical child receiving state disability benefits had a severe physical impairment or mental retardation. These were impairments that effectively required care around the clock and frequently prevented children from attending school and participating in outside activities to the same degree as children without disabilities. These impairments also created substantial costs for families.[3] Although there was considerable debate around the passage of the SSI-disabled children program, the federal government eventually decided it should level the playing field for low-income families with a disabled child by providing access to medical care through Medicaid and access to cash transfers to offset additional expenses and the earnings forgone from providing care around the clock.[4]

Over time, the changing characteristics of the SSI-disabled children population, with respect to both the types of families entering the program and the types of conditions that qualify a child for enrollment, have reignited some of the original concerns raised about the SSI-disabled children program. Research by Hemmeter, Kauff, and Wittenburg (2009) and by Loprest and Wittenburg (2007) suggests that current SSI beneficiaries bear little resemblance to the description of families in need of assistance for disabled children by the National Academy of Social Insurance (Mashaw, Perrin, and Reno 1996).

Along with changes in family composition, the diagnoses of children entering the SSI program have changed. At the program's inception, nearly 40 percent of children entering were diagnosed with mental retardation. The remaining children were diagnosed with pervasive physical disabilities. In contrast, in 2001, only 8 percent of the children in the SSI-disabled children program reported diagnoses of mental retardation, and about 40 percent had pervasive physical disabilities. Increasingly, entrants to the SSI-disabled children program are diagnosed with other mental disorders and behavioral disorders, such as ADHD, or system disorders, such as asthma. While challenging to the children and parents who cope with them, these disorders generally should not prevent parents from working in the labor market in order to provide care for their children.

Growth in the SSI-Disabled Children Program

As shown in chapter 2, the SSI-disabled children program has grown over time both in caseloads and expenditures. However, since the SSI-disabled children program serves only children living in low-income families, to get an accurate picture of growth it is important to adjust these measures relative to the potentially eligible population. Two such adjusted measures, an age-based metric and an income-based metric, are shown in figure 6-1. Figure 6-1 reports the levels and trends in the number of children receiving SSI-disabled children benefits per thousand children under eighteen (age eligible), and the number of children receiving SSI-disabled children benefits per families in poverty (income eligible).[5] These measures provide rough estimates of the changing importance over time of the SSI-disabled children programs to the general population of low-income families with at least one child.

The trends in these two measures confirm the patterns in the caseload and expenditure data—SSI-disabled children caseloads are rising. Similar to the SSI-disabled adults program, the SSI-disabled children caseload as a percentage of the age-eligible population has grown over time, with especially large increases since 1989. Considering the caseloads relative to the population meeting both the age- and income-eligibility guidelines, the growth in caseloads is even more rapid. Program growth was

FIGURE 6-1

SSI-DISABLED CHILDREN CASELOADS PER THOUSAND CHILDREN
AND PER THOUSAND LOW-INCOME CHILDREN OVER TIME

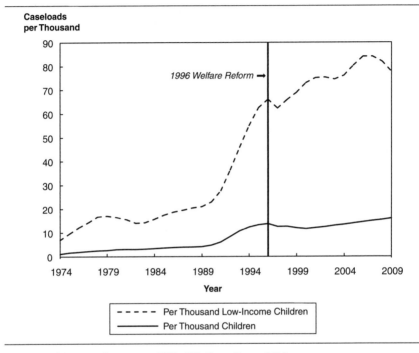

SOURCE: Social Security Administration 2009a; U.S. Census Bureau 2010.

rapid in the 1970s at the program's beginning, and it was followed by relatively slow growth through most of the 1980s. In 1990, caseloads jumped following the Supreme Court decision that expanded eligibility, and continued to rise until 1996. Caseloads per thousand children fell for one year in 1996 before trending upward again.[6] By 2006, over eighty children per thousand age- and income-eligible children were receiving SSI-disabled children benefits. The rate has fallen somewhat in the wake of the recession, but that owes to the outsized increase in the number of low-income children associated with the economy's downturn.

Just as in the SSDI and SSI-disabled adults programs, the important question for SSI-disabled children benefits is what explains the growth.

Three factors are considered: increased prevalence of severe childhood impairments, explicit changes in eligibility rules, and changes in the interpretation and implementation of these rules over time. Although the data on childhood disability and benefit receipt are much more limited than for adults, we address each of these topics with the empirical research available.

Health. As with adults, defining and measuring disability in children is difficult and complicated. Unfortunately, there is also much less empirical information about childhood health and disability than is available for adults. That said, the limited information on trends in child health and functional limitation point to little change over time.[7] Figures 6-2a and 6-2b show two different measures of underlying child health and disability.

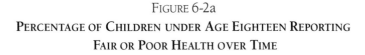

FIGURE 6-2a

PERCENTAGE OF CHILDREN UNDER AGE EIGHTEEN REPORTING
FAIR OR POOR HEALTH OVER TIME

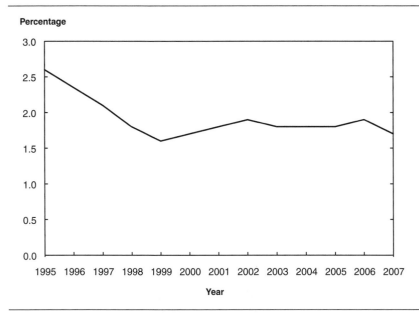

SOURCE: National Center for Health Statistics 2010.

Figure 6-2a shows data on self-assessed health, specifically the percentage of children under age eighteen assessed by parents to be in poor or fair health. Although there is some fluctuation over time, there is no notable upward trend in the prevalence of poor or fair health over time. Figure 6-2b shows the percentage of children ages five to seventeen with an activity limitation by poverty status. Again, the key finding of this figure is that there has been little change over time in functional limitations among any of the populations shown, including those who may be income-eligible. While these data are limited, they provide little indication that changes in child health can explain the enormous variation and growth in the SSI-disabled children rolls relative to the age- and income-eligible population observed in figure 6-1.

FIGURE 6-2b

PERCENTAGE OF CHILDREN AGES FIVE TO SEVENTEEN REPORTING
ACTIVITY LIMITATIONS, BY POVERTY STATUS

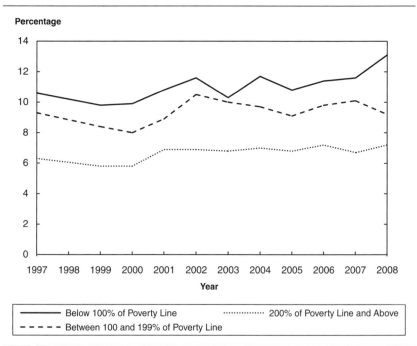

SOURCE: National Center for Health Statistics 2010.

Changing Program Rules. When the SSI-disabled children program was originally considered, Congress recognized the potential difficulties of applying the standard SSA disability definition to children. Thus, under the original legislation, Congress wrote that a child should be considered disabled if "he suffers from any medically determinable physical or mental impairment of comparable severity" to a disabling impairment in an adult. In practice, children originally qualified for SSI if they had "a medically determinable physical or mental impairment which results in marked and severe functional limitations, and which can be expected to result in death, or which has lasted or can be expected to last for a continuous period of not less than 12 months." Between 1974 and 1989, the child disability determination process did not include a functional assessment or account for the equivalent of adult vocational factors. See figure 6-3 for a comparison of the child disability determination process over time.

This changed in 1990, when the U.S. Supreme Court decided the case of *Sullivan v. Zebley*. The Court ruled that to meet the standard of equal treatment, a functional limitation component parallel to that of adults must be included in the initial disability determination process for children. In response, the SSA added two new bases for finding children eligible for benefits: (1) functional equivalence, which was set at the medical-listing level of the disability determination process; and (2) an individualized functional assessment (IFA), which was designed to parallel the vocational assessment provided for adults. By allowing applicants who did not meet the medical listing to be found disabled if their impairments were severe enough to limit their ability to engage in age-appropriate activities, such as attending school, the IFA lowered the level of severity required for children to be eligible for SSI benefits (GAO 1994, 1995).[8]

In 1996, as part of welfare reform, Congress modified the definition of disability for children. Legislators replaced the comparable severity (to adults) criteria with a definition of disability that is unique to children. Under the new definition, a child's impairment—or combination of impairments—is considered disabling only if it results in marked and severe functional limitations, is expected to result in death, or has lasted or can be expected to last at least twelve months. The new focus on assessing the severity of impairments among children was reflected in changes in the evaluation process. The legislation removed the IFA,

FIGURE 6-3

SEQUENTIAL INITIAL DISABILITY DETERMINATION PROCESS FOR CHILDREN

CHILDREN: PRE-ZEBLEY	CHILDREN: POST-ZEBLEY	CHILDREN: POST-1996 WELFARE REFORM
1. Are you working? 　　Y = Deny	1. Are you working? 　　Y = Deny	1. Are you working? 　　Y = Deny
	2. Do you have a severe impairment?[b] 　　Y = Deny	2. Do you have a severe impairment?[d] 　　Y = Deny
Compare Impairment to Medical Listings	**Compare Impairment to Medical Listings**	**Compare Impairment to Medical Listings**
	Mental[c] / Other	Mental[c] / Other
3a. Meet criteria in medical listings? 　　Y = Allow	3a. Meet both diagnostic (A) and functional (B) criteria? 　　Y = Allow / 3a. Medically meet medical listings? 　　Y = Allow	3a. Meet both diagnostic (A) and functional (B) criteria? 　　Y = Allow / 3a. Medically meet medical listings? 　　Y = Allow
3b. Medically equal medical listings?[a] 　　Y = Allow; N = Deny	3b. Equal (meet [B] and some of [A])? 　　Y = Allow / 3b. Medically equal medical listings? 　　Y = Allow	3b. Equal (meet [B] and some of [A])? 　　Y = Allow / 3b. Medically equal medical listings? 　　Y = Allow
	3c. Functionally equal medical listings? 　　Y = Allow	3c. Functionally equal medical listings? 　　Y = Allow
	Individualized Functional Assessment (IFA) 4. Given IFA, is impairment(s) of comparable severity to that which would disable an adult? 　　Y = Allow; N = Deny	

SOURCE: Created by authors using disability determination guidelines in Social Security Administration, various years a.

NOTES: a. Before 1990, SSA policy in SS Ruling 83-19 explicitly prohibited using an overall functional assessment to find that a claimant's impairment equaled the medical listings. A claimant with multiple impairments could meet or equal the listings only if at least one impairment alone met or medically equated a specific listing. b. A medically determinable physical or mental impairment of comparable severity to one meeting the adult definition. c. The childhood mental disorders listings were modified in 1990 to include functional criteria similar to those put in the adult listings in 1985. d. A medically determinable physical or mental impairment that results in marked and severe functional limitation.

replacing it with criteria based on functional equivalence or evaluations of the extent to which impairments meet or exceed medical-listing-level severity. The revised rules defined medical-listing-level severity for functional limitations as: (1) marked limitations in two broad areas of functioning, such as social functioning or personal functioning; or (2) extreme limitations in one area of functioning, such as inability to walk. In practice these changes meant that although functional limitations continued to include behavior-related limitations, they no longer covered the same breadth of functioning included in the IFA. For example, Congress specifically removed maladaptive-behavior disorder from the functional-listing criteria. Thus, the post-1996 standard represents a broader measure of disability than originally applied to children but a narrower standard than the one used between 1990 and 1996 (see figure 6-3).[9]

Applying Changing Rules. It is clear that changes in rules for children applying for SSI had a noticeable effect on caseloads, but the way SSI administrators interpreted these rules also had an impact on the rolls. The outcome of applying more subjective criteria to determine eligibility can be seen in figure 6-4. This figure shows the percentage of SSI-disabled children awards by two conditions: mental retardation and other mental conditions. These conditions represent extremes of the distribution between medically measurable and more subjectively determined. Mental retardation is a long-standing diagnosis with objective measurable criteria that can be applied consistently across evaluators. Mental impairments other than mental retardation are much more difficult to measure objectively.

In 1983, approximately 37 percent of new beneficiaries qualified based on mental retardation and only 5 percent had other mental conditions. By 2003, over one-half of all new beneficiaries listed other mental conditions as their qualifying diagnosis. Part of the explanation for this increase is a specific change in the eligibility criteria—an SSA-based easing of criteria for meeting or exceeding the medical listings for mental impairments and a *Zebley*-based expansion to include functional limitations. Following this change in criteria, the share of new beneficiaries based on a mental condition has continued to grow at a rate much closer to the rapid rate that immediately followed the *Zebley* decision. The increase in the share of new beneficiaries with other mental conditions since *Zebley*, and especially since

FIGURE 6-4
PERCENTAGE OF SSI-DISABLED CHILDREN AWARDS FOR MENTAL RETARDATION
AND FOR OTHER MENTAL CONDITIONS OVER TIME

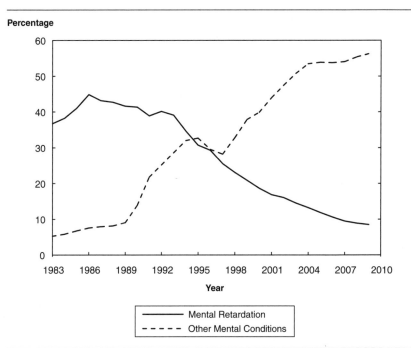

SOURCE: Social Security Administration, various years b.

the efforts to limit entry in 1996, suggests that gatekeeper discretion in determining these outcomes is another driver of SSI-disabled children caseload growth. This influence can be seen in figure 6-5, which shows that awards are increasingly based on functional criteria. The percentage of SSI-disabled children awards based on meeting or equaling the medical listings has declined substantially, and the percentage of children awarded benefits based on functional listings has risen accordingly.

These figures show that changes in program rules (especially the *Zebley* decision), and the subsequent administration of these rules, are affecting program growth. The growth in the SSI-disabled children rolls does not seem consistent with changes in the underlying health conditions among children. Rather, it appears to be based on an increase in applications and

FIGURE 6-5
PERCENTAGE OF DISTRIBUTION OF SSI-DISABLED CHILDREN
BENEFITS BY TYPE OF MEDICAL ALLOWANCE OVER TIME

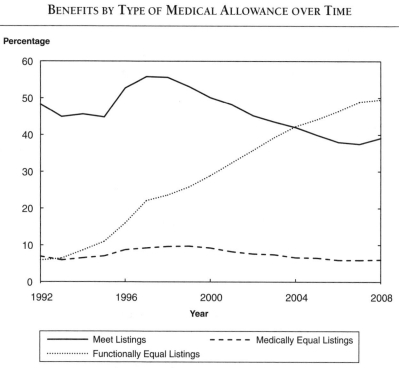

SOURCE: Social Security Administration, various years b.

acceptances onto the rolls that revolves around program eligibility rules and their implementation.

Disability Policy, Welfare Policy, and Disability Decision Making

As we did for the adult disability programs in chapter 4, we show the decision trees for potential candidates to the SSI-disabled children program and for the state agencies with which they interact in figures 6-6a and 6-6b. The first thing to notice is that there is no decision tree for the child in this program. The child's interests are represented by the parent and, to a lesser extent, by the state. While this is reasonable, it means that the decision to apply for SSI-disabled children benefits can be based as much on the family's economic circumstances as on the child's disability and specific needs for care. Indeed, Rupp and Ressler (2009) find that the probability that a parent with a disabled child is working is driven by variables other than the severity of the child's impairment. Figure 6-6a shows that for those who are working at the time of the child's health shock, a parent or parents will be forced to decide whether to leave or reduce employment to care for the child. For the vast majority of Americans with long work histories, stable jobs, health insurance, and family income well above the minimum income protection of the SSI-disabled children program, it is highly unlikely that they will turn to this program for assistance. For the minority of Americans with intermittent work histories, low-paying or unstable jobs, no health insurance, and family incomes near the SSI minimum guarantee, however, the benefits offered first by temporary welfare (AFDC/TANF) and eventually by the SSI-disabled children program are a possible alternative path

FIGURE 6-6a
DECISION TREE FOR LOW-INCOME ADULTS REACTING TO THE ONSET
OF A CHILD'S DISABILITY THAT MIGHT MAKE THEIR HOUSEHOLD ELIGIBLE
FOR SSI-DISABLED CHILDREN BENEFITS

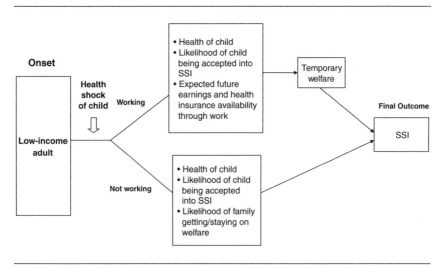

SOURCE: Authors' illustration of the decision making process.

TABLE 6-1
THE CHANGING GAIN FOR SINGLE-MOTHER FAMILIES TRANSFERRING
FROM AFDC/TANF BENEFITS TO SSI, 1996 AND 2005

	AFDC/TANF Benefit, no SSI (in 2005$)		AFDC/TANF/SSI Benefits with One Child on SSI (in 2005$)		Percentage Gain from Transferring One Child to SSI	
	1996	2005	1996	2005	1996	2005
National[a]	468	427	980	956	109.2%	123.8%
National without California[b]	426	371	937	897	119.9	141.9
California[b]	736	786	1250	1330	69.9	69.2
New York[c]	713	577	1187	1103	66.6	91.2
Texas	232	223	782	772	236.7	246.2

SOURCE: Wiseman 2010, table 2.
NOTES: Benefits are as of July 1; dollar amounts are in 2005 dollars.
  a. Average across states weighted by current TANF caseload.
  b. California data are for Los Angeles. The increase in real benefits between 1996 and 2005 in California is attributable to that state's special treatment of households exempt from TANF work requirements.
  c. New York data are for New York City.

given a child's unexpected health shock.[10] In such cases, the child's impairment will certainly affect this decision, but so will the likelihood that the child will be eligible for SSI-disabled children program benefits and their future earnings and private access to health care. As Hemmeter, Kauff, and Wittenburg (2009) and Loprest and Wittenburg (2007) show, however, such children are much more likely to live with a single parent, and less than half of those single parents are employed. Thus, the majority of SSI-disabled children household beneficiaries likely do not have a working member at the onset of the child's impairment.

Figure 6-6a also shows that for a parent who is not working at the time a child experiences a health shock, decisions need to be made that will be affected by the child's health and likelihood of being found eligible for SSI-disabled children benefits. In addition, the family must determine whether there is a financial gain to qualifying for SSI over staying on the more general welfare program. Table 6-1 shows the relative financial gain for the average single-mother family on AFDC in 1996 if a mother were able to qualify her child for the SSI-disabled children program. In such a

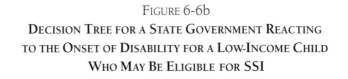

FIGURE 6-6b
DECISION TREE FOR A STATE GOVERNMENT REACTING
TO THE ONSET OF DISABILITY FOR A LOW-INCOME CHILD
WHO MAY BE ELIGIBLE FOR SSI

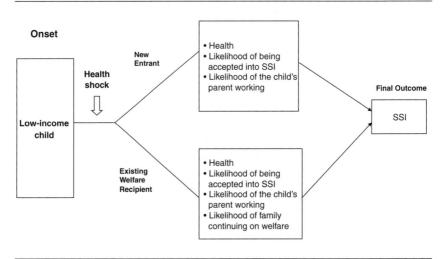

SOURCE: Authors' illustration of the decision making process.

case, she would have nearly doubled her cash transfers. The gain was highest in states like Texas, where AFDC benefits were relatively low compared to SSI-disabled children benefits, but gains were still fairly large in states like California and New York, which had higher AFDC benefits but also offered state supplements to the federal SSI-disabled children payment. After welfare reform, the average gains were even larger.

This understates the long-term gains to such single mothers because, under TANF, the mother is guaranteed only five years of benefits and is under other pressures to work. Under the SSI-disabled children program, benefits continue until the child turns eighteen, and the parent is not expected to work. Evidence suggests that a large fraction of the children enrolling in the SSI-disabled children program in the 1990s previously participated in the AFDC program. Empirical research examining the degree to which these relative gains produced this shift from AFDC/TANF to the SSI-disabled children program has found it to be significant (Garrett and Glied 2000; Kubik 1999). While it is difficult to identify the effect of this type of incentive, one paper (Kubik 1999) finds that reported disabilities by newly awarded SSI-disabled children—particularly mental impairments, which as we have discussed are the most difficult to objectively evaluate—were higher in states with lower AFDC benefits, where the relative gains from movement onto the SSI-disabled children program were higher.

Figure 6-6b shows that states will also make decisions that influence whether a family that is either applying for state welfare benefits or already on them chooses to apply for SSI-disabled children benefits. Like the parent, the state will consider the child's health and the likelihood the child will be accepted into the program. The state will also consider whether the parent is a good candidate for employment. In the case of single mothers, it is in the interest of the state not only to encourage their AFDC/TANF population to apply for SSI benefits, but also to provide resources for them to do so. In chapter 4, we discussed the incentives states have to move their adult welfare population to the SSI-disabled adults program, since this would shift the responsibility of providing cash transfers for those adults to the federal government and reduce any cost the state would absorb in trying to encourage employment. This is also the case for the SSI-disabled children program. While AFDC/TANF single mothers who are able-bodied are not candidates for the SSI-disabled adults program, their income maintenance would be guaranteed by the federal government if their child were eligible for the SSI-disabled children program. To the degree that children with some level of impairment made it more difficult to encourage single mothers to join the workforce, the SSI-disabled children program is the only other avenue for reducing the burden they place on state revenues.

Although the SSI-disabled children program was intended as an income-support program for families headed by parents who were unable to work because of their child's disability, it appears to have grown into an income maintenance program for low-income families with a qualifying child. This has altered the incentives of all actors in ways that likely affect outcomes including caseloads, costs, and ultimately the long-run economic status of the child. At each point in the process that leads parents to apply for SSI-disabled children benefits, decisions have to be made by both parents and the states that provide services to these families before they move further along the path to long-term benefits. The eligibility rules facing SSI-disabled children and how the system is financed influences the behavior of parents of disabled children and the states in which they live in their response to a child's health shock.

Unintended Consequences and Long-Term Costs

In addition to the program costs of the SSI-disabled children program and the inefficiency of delivering benefits to low-income families based on a child's disability, research on the SSI-disabled children population points to potential long-term costs of this program. One concern is that a substantial fraction of children on the SSI-disabled children program move directly to the SSI-disabled adults program without attempting to enter the labor market. Hemmeter, Kauff, and Wittenburg (2009) find that nearly two-thirds of these children transition directly to the SSI-adult disability rolls. Once this transition is complete, very few attempt to work thereafter. Moreover, of those who do not move directly onto the rolls, only about 60 percent are employed at age nineteen (Hemmeter, Kauff, and Wittenburg 2009). Thus, most SSI-disabled children beneficiaries age out of this program into what is likely to be a permanent life on the SSI-disabled adults program or, in the event of denial of SSI-disabled adults benefits, turn to other forms of social welfare.

This outcome is costly both to the beneficiaries who live their lives at or near the poverty threshold and to taxpayers who are funding the benefits. In April 2005, approximately 776,000 youth ages fourteen through twenty-five were receiving either SSI-disabled children or SSI-disabled adults benefits totaling more than $4 billion each year (MDRC 2008). The cost of providing such a low level of economic well-being to a growing number of young adults, most of whom have aged onto the SSI-disabled adults rolls, has raised concerns among policymakers (Social Security Advisory Board 2006) and resulted in a large-scale attempt by the SSA to support work among young adults on the SSI-disabled adults program (SSA Youth Transition Demonstration Project n.d.). Although such efforts are warranted, given the number of children who stay on the program throughout their lives, these efforts, which primarily focus on these youth after they have come onto the SSI-disabled adults rolls, again highlight the counterintuitive approach to U.S. disability policy, in which adult benefits are awarded based on an inability to perform any substantial gainful activity before these same new beneficiaries are encouraged, but not required, to work.

Summary

This chapter has shown that the substantial growth in the share of the age- and income-eligible population of children receiving SSI-disabled children benefits is more likely the result of program changes—the expansion in the eligibility criteria for program entry and the administration of these expanded eligibility standards by SSA gatekeepers—than of changes in the overall health of children. While this program growth was trimmed initially by an explicit tightening of program eligibility standards associated with welfare reform in 1996, an unintended consequence of welfare reform is that it creates incentives for states to shift single mothers who have disabled children to the SSI-disabled children program. This makes it more likely that these children will simply age onto the SSI-disabled adults program.

7

Reforming U.S. Disability Policy

The passage of the Americans with Disabilities Act in 1990 produced considerable optimism about the integration of people with disabilities into the labor market. However, twenty years later, and despite progress on removing social and physical barriers, the employment rates of those with disabilities are lower, not higher, and their household incomes have remained flat in real terms and fallen relative to the rest of the working-age population. Moreover, a growing share of the population with disabilities has become dependent on government transfers, a fact that threatens the financial viability of these systems.

We have argued that these outcomes owe more to policy than to health, and as such were not inevitable. While the ADA changed the law regarding the treatment of people with disabilities, the safety net aimed at protecting their economic status—SSDI and SSI—remained the same, leaving it out of sync with the goals and expectations embodied in the ADA. Today, SSDI and SSI programs continue to substitute for, and thus discourage, work—directly, through program rules, and indirectly, through the signals sent to employers and the state governments who help determine how a disabled person will respond at the onset of a health condition.

Based on lessons learned from U.S. welfare reform and Dutch disability reform, in this chapter we sketch out the elements of structural reforms intended to align the SSDI and SSI programs more closely with the stated goals of the ADA.

Learning from Welfare Reform

The experience of reforming the U.S. welfare system provides several useful observations for thinking about SSDI and SSI. Among the most important is that individuals respond to financial and institutional incentives embedded purposely or unintentionally in public programs. As such, an observation of behavior, such as not working, does not necessarily indicate that the behavior (work) is not possible. In the case of single mothers, changes in the incentives following welfare reform led to substantial changes in employment and to observers' realization that the population of single mothers was much more capable of working than previously thought. Another important lesson from this program change is that when policies promote work and make work profitable, many individuals and their families can maintain or exceed the economic status provided by a cash-benefit system.

Welfare reform also teaches about the process of changing public policy. As described in chapter 2, the reforms to the old model of welfare provision happened slowly. States originally led the way through waivers that allowed them to move away from federal regulations and try new service delivery mechanisms and innovative programs. These state initiatives provided data from which to build the federal welfare rules and on which to base best practices for other states to use when crafting their own programs under full devolution. This experimentation phase was critical to the rapid and successful deployment of state policies following the federal reforms. In thinking about disability policy reforms, it seems prudent to have a similar multiphase plan that first collects evidence about reforms that do and do not work.[1]

Finally, welfare reform demonstrates that programs with well-managed incentives in place can act as their own gatekeeping system, meaning that individuals, employers, and states self-select who can and cannot work and make judgments accordingly. Under this design, it is more plausible that those remaining on public programs are unable to work and in need of some form of nonwork-based public assistance. Since those who can work already will have opted to do so, the programs designed for the remaining nonworking population will be long-term support programs with no expectation of, requirement for, or investment in its beneficiaries' ability to move off the rolls over their lifetimes.[2]

Learning from the Dutch Disability Reforms

Disability policy reform in the Netherlands offers another useful set of experiences from which to borrow. The Dutch faced many of the same pressures as the United States with respect to disability policy: rapid growth in the rolls, unsustainable growth in expenditures, and a mix of incentives that produced these outcomes. The Dutch also had a long history of trying to reform their program. A key lesson from those experiences is that attempts to reform the system by lowering benefit levels and tightening eligibility rules lead to reductions in the program population, but are not sufficient to solve the problem of growing and expensive disability rolls. The more structural reforms in 2002 that shifted the incentives of both employees and their employers, resulting in greater investment of time and effort in improving work outcomes following the onset of a disability, to date have been able to curb growth in the Dutch disability system.

The second important lesson from the Dutch experience is that disability program rules, the administration of those rules, and the methods established to pay for these programs greatly influence the behavior of key actors—employees and employers—at the time a worker experiences the onset of a disability. This mirrors some of the lessons learned from U.S. welfare reform and underscores the idea that behavior responds to program design. Taking this insight to policy, the Dutch were able to change their programs so both employers and employees bore the costs of the disability program more directly. The result was a different mix of accommodation, rehabilitation, and cash transfers that resulted in fewer workers moving onto the disability cash-transfer rolls. This leads to the third lesson from the Dutch experience: signaling to agents (employers, insurers, gatekeepers, and individuals) the true cost of moving individuals with disabilities onto long-term cash-transfer rolls will slow down the flow of applicants to these programs and increase the amount of accommodation and employment support available to those who suffer a health shock.

Reforming U.S. Disability Policy

Most would agree that caseloads and costs for U.S. disability programs are rising at an unsustainable pace. The Social Security Trustees and the Congressional Budget Office estimate the SSDI system will be insolvent in 2018 (CBO 2010b; SSA 2010a). Previous attempts at SSDI and SSI policy reform in the United States have succeeded in controlling program growth only temporarily. Reforms started by the Carter administration and vigorously pursued by the Reagan administration in the early 1980s—during a severe economic recession—were extremely controversial and resulted in a backlash that made it nearly impossible to remove current beneficiaries from the disability rolls. As discussed in chapter 3, subsequent SSDI policies that made entry into the program easier have resulted in U.S. caseloads that, in 2009, exceeded eighty per thousand workers, twice the level they reached before the system-expansion policies of the mid-1980s and greater than that of the Netherlands (figure 5-1). In 2009 and again in 2010, application rates for SSDI reached historic highs (figure 3-4). In all likelihood, this will produce calls for program reforms to end the crisis in rising program costs. Rather than simply returning to policy changes taken up in the 1980s, we argue that more systemic solutions should be considered. The remainder of the chapter lays out a framework for this type of reform to U.S. disability policy.

Prioritizing Work. Based on the importance of work to the long-term economic status of working-age people, our primary recommendation is that policymakers adopt a work-first strategy for people with disabilities. Based on the ability of U.S. welfare reform and Dutch disability reform to increase the employment rates of their respective target populations, we suggest that changing U.S. disability policy to promote work has the potential to produce a similar outcome. At a minimum, this would mean bringing the SSA investments in work currently targeted only on those already on the SSDI or SSI rolls to all disabled individuals applying for benefits. Doing so will eliminate the need for the counterintuitive policy currently in place in which the SSA provides access to work-focused support only after applicants for SSDI or SSI benefits have gone through an extended process of demonstrating that they are unable to work (see figure 7-1a). Beginning

FIGURE 7-1a
SSA's CURRENT MODEL

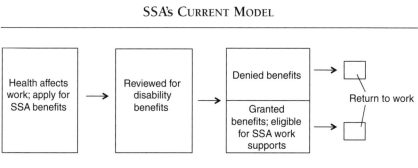

SOURCE: Authors' illustration of current disability model.

SSA policy interventions with employment-oriented supports as figure 7-1b outlines can improve a range of problems burdening the disability system. Importantly, work-first strategies are consistent with the goals of the ADA, which called for the integration of people with disabilities into the labor market. They also provide a long-term opportunity for people with disabilities to reap some of the rewards of a growing economy, an opportunity not granted by the current cash-benefit system. Moreover, SSA work-oriented approaches that make the returns to employment higher than cash benefits will assist SSA program administrators in determining who is more plausibly unable to work, thus limiting growth in the rolls caused by changes in enforcement or measurement issues. Finally, SSA work-first efforts for children on the SSI-disabled children program could, if successful, help move these children into the workforce as they get older, where they will have access to the full social safety net provided by SSDI if they eventually become unable to work.

Even these types of SSA-based work-first initiatives will often come too late in the process following the onset of a disability to be effective and would require the SSA to develop an expertise in disability case management that it currently lacks. More systemic policy changes, like the Dutch reforms, would provide much clearer signals to the primary actors who do have such experience and can make case-management decisions immediately following the onset of disability: employers and states.

FIGURE 7-1b
PROPOSED EARLY-INTERVENTION MODEL

SOURCE: Authors' illustration of proposed disability model.

Separating Disability Insurance from Welfare for Those with Disabilities. As we have described in this book, the two major disability programs in the United States (SSDI and SSI) are dissimilar in every way except that the SSA is responsible for evaluating who is eligible to participate in both programs. With this in mind, we propose leaving the SSDI, an insurance program, under the SSA and devolving the SSI welfare program to states. Our proposed division of authority would be more consistent with the general policy framework in the United States of distinguishing welfare from insurance programs. This division would also help minimize the counterproductive incentives currently in place that motivate states to shift costs to the federal government by shifting applicants from welfare to disability programs. Finally, it would allow the SSA to focus more attention on the insurance program, SSDI, and on working to improve efforts to promote work, accommodation, and rehabilitation activities that are part of the activities of private insurance firms acting as agents for employers with respect to WC and employer-provided, long-term private insurance programs.

Reforming SSDI

Both the Government Accountability Office and, more recently, the Social Security Advisory Board have criticized the SSA's management practices (GAO 1997; Daub 2002). Some of this criticism relates to issues discussed in this book, and some is much more detailed with respect to SSA's difficulty in determining whether applicants are eligible for benefits. Most researchers can agree improved management practices are necessary; chief among them is to establish standard eligibility criteria for gatekeepers and the administrative law judges to use. In addition, the application and appeals system should be made more equitable; both the SSA and applicants should be able to provide evidence before judges in the appeals process. Eligibility standards must be clarified for conditions that are difficult to determine, particularly for the mental illness and musculoskeletal conditions that have propelled much of the growth in SSDI, as discussed in chapter 3.

It is unlikely that marginal changes in SSDI program management or disability standards will have much effect in slowing the pace of SSDI growth; more fundamental changes need to be made. The most popular current proposals for SSDI reform focus on increasing the work effort of those already on the SSDI rolls and would likely make only a marginal difference (if any) in SSDI growth. One portion of that popular reform would address current earnings limitations for SSDI beneficiaries.[3] These limitations clearly discourage current beneficiaries from working above the substantial gainful activity restriction ($1,000 per month in 2010), since to do so would eventually result in the loss of all SSDI benefits. Raising this limit or allowing beneficiaries to permanently earn wage and salary income above this amount with only a partial loss of SSDI benefits would increase their employment marginally—thereby reducing program costs to the degree that lower benefits would be paid—but this reform would almost certainly be offset by an increase in the number of new beneficiaries. It would encourage applicants because it would allow beneficiaries to work while staying on the program after they had demonstrated an inability to work in the application process. The effect of this marginal change in SSDI rules, if any, would be to increase program costs and caseloads and to make beneficiaries less likely to receive the accommodations that could prevent them from enrolling in the first place.

A common component of all SSA-initiated work interventions is a focus on current beneficiaries. This reflects rules requiring SSA-collected funds to be focused on current program recipients. Thus, the SSA is forced to focus its work strategies on SSDI beneficiaries rather than on workers with limitations who are trying to decide whether to stay on the job or apply for benefits. Unfortunately, as both U.S. welfare reform and the Dutch disability policy reforms showed, the most effective place to slow program growth is at the entry point. This is not a new perspective. It is well known among gatekeepers in the private disability insurance system and, we argue, must be at the heart of all serious efforts to stem the tide of new beneficiaries to the SSDI program. The question is how to do it.

Experience Rating SSDI. As chapters 3 and 4 demonstrated, our current system of funding SSDI via a flat-rate payroll tax on employers and employees fails to send the appropriate signals to them with respect to the full costs of a worker moving from the work path to the permanent disability path. In contrast, using experience rating to determine a firm's per-worker tax rate for SSDI would more directly link the costs to the firm of one of its workers moving onto the SSDI program, and thereby require an employer to balance the full economic costs and benefits of providing accommodation and rehabilitation versus assisting a worker onto the SSDI program following a health shock. Under the current cost structure, the federal government pays for the additional SSDI beneficiary, which simultaneously frees the employer from bearing the costs associated with accommodation and rehabilitation. If employers bore the costs for both options an employee with a disability might choose, they might be more interested in making investments in accommodation and rehabilitation that could prolong the employment tenure of a worker with a disability than in simply encouraging employees to take the permanent disability path. Effective accommodation and rehabilitation options would likely delay the movement of some workers with a disability onto the SSDI rolls.

As we showed in chapter 5, the reforms to the Dutch disability system greatly increased the likelihood that individuals with disabilities would continue to work and delay moving onto disability benefits. One key component of these reforms was to make employers more directly bear the cost of moving their employees onto long-term disability insurance benefits. While the United States is unlikely to adopt the mandate that forced Dutch employers to take responsibility for their employees' post-disability well-being, we argue that it is important for firms and workers to more clearly recognize the additional burden their behavior currently places on the SSDI system. Because U.S. employers incur no additional costs when their workers move onto the SSDI rolls, they do not recognize the real cost incurred when they deny accommodation, rehabilitation, and return-to-work efforts. Similarly, employers who do provide safe workplaces or accommodation to their workers following the onset of a disability receive no direct cost benefit for this behavior in regard to SSDI taxes.

One way to make employers recognize these added costs is to use experience rating for SSDI employer taxes by raising the tax on firms whose workers enroll in the system at above-average rates and lowering the SSDI taxes on firms whose workers enroll at below-average rates. This is currently the system used to fund state unemployment insurance and WC benefits, and using best practices from these state programs could be considered for disability benefits as well.[4] Alternatively, employers who provide some set of short-term private disability insurance for employees and whose private insurance agents cooperate with SSDI gatekeepers in managing their cases could be granted a reduction in SSDI tax rates, while firms that did not offer such private insurance could be charged a higher SSDI tax rate. Each of these reforms would make employers more likely to provide greater accommodation and rehabilitation to their workers immediately following the onset of a disability. This same kind of fundamental policy change was behind the reforms of Dutch disability policy in 2002. Doing so not only would bend the cost curve of projected SSDI program expenditures by reducing incentives for employers and employees to overuse the system, but would increase the employment of working-age people with disabilities as well as their income.

Can Experience Rating Work? The evidence from the Netherlands' disability insurance reforms suggests that some form of experience rating could substantially slow the movement of workers onto the SSDI rolls following the onset of a work limitation. Burkhauser, Schmeiser, and Weathers (forthcoming), show that American employers were more likely to provide accommodations to their workers following the onset of work limitation when it occurred on the job and, hence, was more likely to be subject to experience rating. But the evidence base for experience rating is not yet strong enough to recommend the immediate implementation of such a major change in SSDI policy. However, it is strong enough that policymakers should require the SSA to shift its demonstration funding away from testing the efficacy of policy options focused on encouraging those currently on the SSDI rolls to leave. Instead, these funds should be used to test the efficacy of experience rating or other policies that would increase the use of accommodation and rehabilitation well before workers apply for SSDI benefits, and thereby slow their movement onto the SSDI rolls.

Berkowitz and Burton (1970) and Burton and Berkowitz (1971) provide the first systematic set of efficiency arguments for experience rating in the context of WC. They argue that experience rating will result in optimal expenditure by firms on safety, accident prevention, and health procedures since the employer would bear the costs of these events more systematically. The result would be fewer accidents. Experience rating will also allocate the costs of disability to the source of the injury more clearly. Thus, firms whose workers require more WC benefits and medical services would pay higher premiums. This direct relationship between the benefits received by a firm's workers and the premiums the firm pays encourages firms to provide the optimal amount of accommodation and rehabilitation and thus reduces transfer payments and ensures greater return to work by injured workers.[5] More germane to SSDI policy reform, Berkowitz and Burton argue that if nonwork-related movements to the SSDI program were randomly distributed across workers, a payroll tax composed of a flat-rate tax together with an experience-rated tax would be socially efficient.

Critics of experience rating are justified in arguing that, perversely, its net impact could be a decrease in employment and an increase in the use of SSDI by working-age people with disabilities. If the risk of a non-job-related, work-limiting condition is not random across all workers but can instead be estimated in advance, then employers might consider workers with these risky characteristics more expensive to hire. This could lead to statistical discrimination. If this form of employer behavior were not illegal or, if illegal, not sufficiently enforced, then the reduction in the hiring of these workers—for example, workers who had disabilities prior to employment—could offset the positive effects of experience rating on the accommodation of currently employed workers and reduce the overall employment of impaired workers while increasing their use of SSDI.

This is a generic criticism of all labor protection laws. In the face of uneven enforcement, any protection given to current workers will subject future workers to reduced employment. Generally, however, the positive employment effects of such labor laws have been found to dominate possible negative effects. For example, Donohue and Heckman (1991) review the literature on the impact of the Civil Rights Act of 1964 on employment and find the net employment effects of this protection against racial discrimination were positive and large. The net impact of the passage of the ADA on the employment of working-age men with disabilities is more controversial. While DeLeire (2000) and Acemoglu and Angrist (2001) find a net negative effect, Houtenville and Burkhauser (2005a) show that the Acemoglu and Angrist results are sensitive to the definition of disability used, and Goodman and Waidmann (2003) argue that the recession and expansion of SSI and SSDI that occurred concurrently with the implementation of the ADA confound these results. (See Burkhauser and Stapleton [2003] for a more detailed discussion.) But even if there is some negative employment effect related to preexisting conditions for potential new hires, it is still possible to offset this effect by, for instance, excluding from harm employers who hire a worker with an identifiable high risk of being able to meet or exceed the medical listings by not including such workers in the pool on which experience ratings are determined.

Although there is insufficient research to justify moving forward with experience rating nationally today, the idea that building a system that allows employers and employees to see the full cost of their decisions remains. The current method for funding SSDI that allows employees, employers, and private insurance agents to pass the costs of long-term cash transfers to the federal government is unsustainable. Moreover, if firms bore the costs more directly, it would likely result in more workers receiving from employers the level of accommodation and rehabilitation they need in order to continue working. The most straightforward way to overcome this flaw is to ensure that those best able to provide the mix of accommodation, rehabilitation, and access to short- and long-term disability cash transfers to workers following the onset of a disability have the correct cost signals to make these decisions efficiently. For SSDI, this might be achieved by giving workers, employers, and private insurers these same signals via experience-rated employer premiums.

Reforming SSI

Previous chapters suggested that the SSI-disabled adults and SSI-disabled children programs closely resemble general welfare programs in the United States and, thus, can be changed using many of the same principles applied in moving from AFDC to TANF. This would mean moving jurisdiction of the SSI-disabled adults and children programs from the SSA to the states.[6] Unlike the previous periods when SSI-like programs were in state hands, this devolution would, like TANF, hold states accountable to federal guidelines regarding outcomes of people with disabilities. Like TANF, these two SSI programs could be funded by block grants from the federal government, and states could be asked to comply with broad goals.[7] At the same time, states would be allowed and encouraged to innovate and create work-based alternatives to long-term cash support for applicants with disabilities. Here we present the details of a framework for implementing this change in the children and adults programs.

The SSI-Disabled Adults Program. One straightforward way to change the SSI-disabled adults program is to borrow from the lessons of welfare reform and devolve it to the states, funded by block grants from the federal government. Doing so would not only remove the incentive for states to shift costs by moving low-income adults who are the most difficult to employ to the federal SSI program but, as discussed in chapter 4, it would also encourage them to provide the same incentives to work as they currently provide single mothers. Treating SSI funds in the same way TANF funds are treated and allowing states the flexibility to spend across programs as they choose would give states greater incentives to invest in more work-oriented assistance for low-income populations, even those with disabilities. While we are not arguing that time limits should be placed on this adult population with disabilities, states should be given some latitude to experiment with penalties for those in this population who do not cooperate with work plans. This devolution would immediately change the focus from providing long-term, low-level cash benefits to people with disabilities not expected to work to providing training, rehabilitation, and work support to individuals who, with proper assistance, likely could and would work.

Just as with welfare reform, an earnings subsidy, like the Earned Income Tax Credit, would be necessary to make it possible for many of these individuals to work. Expanding the EITC to individuals with disabilities who integrate into the labor market is an important component of any disability policy reform. Not only would the EITC assist individuals in making work pay, but it would also give states the added incentive to assist their citizens with disabilities in finding and keeping employment. Since the EITC is federally funded, its use would increase the cash inflow to marginal populations in the state without dipping into state revenues.[8]

The SSI-Disabled Children Program. Following welfare reform, and in keeping with the changing views about the integration of children with disabilities into the schools, we suggest that families of children in the SSI-disabled children program be placed under the case management of state welfare agencies and that states use the same mix of supports (for example, child care and job training) and requirements (such as potential loss of benefits for noncooperation) to encourage working-age adults in these families to work. States would be able to use their funds to better target the special needs of the children with disabilities in these families.[9] States would also be able to use these funds to provide services, rather than cash, to children with disabilities directly. These services could be refined to match the specific needs of the local population and, ideally, to improve the long-run ability of these children to enter the labor force.

These types of changes would move toward solving a number of the issues raised in chapter 6. First, on equity grounds, placing responsibility for all welfare families with the states would reduce the difference in treatment of poor families based on whether they have children who meet the SSI-disabled children standards. Second, devolving the SSI-disabled children program to the states would limit states' incentives to shift the costs of managing welfare caseloads to the federal government through the SSI system. Finally, because states would carry the full burden of children with disabilities who remained in their welfare population once they reached working age, they would have a much greater incentive to provide the education, training, and accommodation necessary to enable children with disabilities to enter the workforce as adults.

Can States Manage the SSI Programs? State welfare agencies now have over a decade of experience in moving welfare mothers and other welfare clients into the workforce. Although this would be a significant change from the last thirty years, and one that states may not want to undertake in a time of severe budget pressures, we argue that it makes sense to integrate the SSI population into the broader state-run social safety net for low-income residents. Providing states with block grants to use for all of their low-income populations has the potential to generate more experimentation and work-oriented programs, including rehabilitation, job training, and accommodation efforts focused on individuals with disabilities. If augmented by the same federal commitments given to low-income single mothers, such as the EITC, child tax credits, and health insurance, states will likely be willing and efficient managers.

Summary

This book has documented the declining work, increasing benefit receipt, and static economic welfare of Americans with disabilities over the past three decades. We have argued that these outcomes are disappointing and not inevitable, owing more to policy than to health. While the ADA helped to remove barriers to work for people with disabilities, a series of policy initiatives designed to increase the nonwork social safety net for people with disabilities decreased their incentives to seek or maintain employment. As a result, the federal disability transfer programs, including SSDI, SSI-disabled adults, and SSI-disabled children, have made work increasingly less desirable for a large share of working-age people with disabilities and less profitable for a growing fraction of able-bodied, low-income parents of children with disabilities. Consequently, the share of adults with disabilities receiving either SSDI or SSI-disabled adults benefits has grown tremendously, as has the share of poor children with disabilities receiving SSI-disabled children benefits. These policy outcomes are costly to taxpayers and to those with disabilities.

As such, we have suggested that fundamental structural changes, similar to the ones that changed U.S. welfare policy and Dutch disability policy, are required. While our outline for change is just a start, the idea that many more—if not most—people with disabilities can work is at least twenty years old. Recognizing this idea and successfully incorporating it into U.S. disability benefit policy will shrink caseloads, curb costs, and improve the opportunities and economic status of people with disabilities.

Data Appendix

Sample Definitions

The sample we use includes all individuals in the March Current Population Survey data who do not have a household member in the military and who are not residing in group quarters. *Working-age individuals* refers to all individuals between the ages of twenty-five and fifty-nine. The working-age population is often defined as persons ages eighteen to sixty-four in published statistics. We use a narrower definition because of the large number of persons ages eighteen to twenty-four whose primary activity is education and the large number of persons ages sixty to sixty-four who are retired. Unless otherwise indicated, the sample used in all tables and figures is the working-age sample.

In most cases, households in the CPS contain one family. For households that contain multiple families related by blood or marriage, we treat subfamilies as separate families for the identification of family structure. Single mothers are defined as women who are not currently married and who are subfamily heads who live with their own never married child(ren) under eighteen. This accounts for important changes in living arrangements, such as the rise in single mothers living with their own parents. As London (1998) notes, prior to 1984 the CPS surveys did not properly account for the household relationships of children living in multigenerational households, producing an undercount of the number of single mothers due to misidentification of those who lived with their parents. To reduce the effect of undercounting this key family type in the early portion of our sample, we applied London's correction to pre-1984 data. If there is a child in the household classified as "other relative of head" and a woman who meets London's criteria (at least fifteen years older than the child and unmarried), then that woman is considered a single mother in our sample.

The population with disabilities includes all individuals who report having "a health problem or a disability which prevents work or which limits the kind or amount of work" they can do. While the use of a work limitation variable to capture the working-age population with disabilities is controversial, the CPS is the only data set that provides a consistent set of questions that allows long-term evaluations of this population. For that reason, it has been widely used in the economics literature to determine the employment and economic well-being of working-age people with disabilities. See, for example, Acemoglu and Angrist (2001); Autor and Duggan (2003); Bound and Waidmann (2002); Burkhauser, Daly, and Houtenville (2001); Burkhauser, Daly, Houtenville, and Nargis (2002); Burkhauser, Houtenville, and Rovba (2009); Daly and Burkhauser (2003); Hotchkiss (2003, 2004); Houtenville and Burkhauser (2005b); and Jolls and Prescott (2005).

In 2008, after a decade of study, the Bureau of Labor Statistics introduced a new six-question sequence of questions into the CPS-Basic Monthly Survey (BMS) for the purpose of determining the working-age population with disabilities. This set of six questions does not include the traditional work-limitation question which the March CPS-Annual Social and Economic Supplement (ASEC) has used since 1981 and which we use in the statistics we report above and in the rest of the book. Burkhauser, Houtenville, and Tennant (2011), using data from both the BMS and ASEC components of the CPS, show that levels of employment and income of this six-question-based disability population are substantially higher and their SSDI- and SSI-program participation is substantially lower than those outcomes when using the work-limitation question to determine this population. This is the case in large part because these six questions only capture 63 percent of the CPS population that reports receiving SSDI or SSI benefits. Once the work-limitation question is added, the new seven-question-based disability population captures 92 percent of the SSDI-SSI population in the CPS. For a discussion of the controversy surrounding the use of CPS data to capture the working-age population with disabilities see Hale (2001), Burkhauser, Daly,

Houtenville, and Nagris (2002), and Burkhauser, Houtenville, and Tennant (2011).

The vulnerable populations compared in this book are single mothers, men with disabilities, and women with disabilities. Disabled single mothers are double counted, because they are included both as single mothers and as women with disabilities.

Business Cycles

The beginning and ending years of a business cycle are somewhat arbitrary. Rather than define them directly by changes in macroeconomic growth, we define them by peaks in median household income, which, in general, lag macroeconomic growth. The peak year is defined as the highest median household income year within a given business cycle, and the trough year is defined as the lowest median household income year within a given business cycle. Our findings are not sensitive to reasonable changes to the peak years we chose to compare. We also provide NBER-defined recession periods in appropriate figures.

Income Measures

Household income is the sum of income for each household member age fifteen and older in the household unit. Negative household income values are recoded as $1. Household income data from the CPS include wages and salaries, self-employment income, property income (interest, dividends, and rents), money-transfer payments from a variety of government and private welfare and social insurance schemes (such as social security, unemployment and workers' compensation, and public assistance), private and government retirement income, interpersonal transfers (such as alimony and child support), and other periodic income. It excludes capital gains and in-kind transfer payments. It does not subtract taxes paid or add tax credits received, so it does not include EITC benefits or the value of food stamps or health services.

It should be noted that income statistics in the CPS refer to receipts during the preceding calendar year, while demographic characteristics, such as age, family or household composition, and work limitation status, are as of the survey date. Therefore, those who became disabled during the survey year are reporting their current disability status while reporting income for the previous year when they were not work limited, potentially biasing our measure of the income for the population with disabilities upward.

Household income does not include amounts received by people who were members during all or part of the income year if these people no longer resided in the household at the time of interview. However, the CPS does collect income data for people who are current residents but who did not reside in the household during the income year.

Income is adjusted for inflation using the Urban Consumer Price Index (CPI-U) estimated by the Bureau of Labor Statistics. Unless otherwise indicated, all incomes reported are pretax, post-transfer income adjusted for inflation to 2008 dollars.

To determine size-adjusted household income for each individual in the household, the total household income is divided by the square root of the number of household members. This is a standard way of controlling for differences in household size in the economic well-being literature. It assumes that the income needed to achieve a given level of economic well-being is lower for those who share a household than for those who live in separate households. See Burkhauser, Smeeding, and Merz (1996) for a discussion of the sensitivity of measures of economic well-being to changes in the measure of returns to scale. All these assumptions with respect to household size adjusted income of persons are standard in the cross national income inequality literature (see Atkinson, Rainwater, and Smeeding [1995]). For a more recent example of their use see Burkhauser, Feng, Jenkins, and Larrimore (forthcoming).

Labor earnings include wages and salary, self-employment, and farm income. Public-assistance income includes compensation from AFDC and General Assistance programs, while food stamps and SSI payments are specifically excluded.

Employment Measures

An individual is considered employed if he or she has worked at least 200 hours during the previous year unless otherwise noted. The employment rate is the percentage of individuals who were employed.

An individual is considered to be living in a working household if the total number of hours worked by members of the household in the previous year was at least 200 hours.

U.S. Program Caseloads and Costs

Social Security Disability Insurance caseloads data on disabled workers are obtained from the Social Security Administration's Office of the Chief Actuary. The numbers are based on the number of beneficiaries in the program on December 31 of the report year. Disabled-worker beneficiaries are, by definition, under the full retirement age (FRA), as they are automatically transferred to the retirement program when they reach FRA.

SSDI program costs include benefit payments to disabled workers and their dependents and administrative expenses. Data on benefit payments and administrative expenses are obtained from the SSA's Office of the Chief Actuary and do not reflect adjustments made for earlier periods.

Supplemental Security Income caseloads data are obtained from various SSI Annual Statistical Reports, which tabulate recipients of federally administered payments. The numbers are based on the number of recipients on the program in December. We define SSI-disabled children as the recipients of federally administered payments who are under the age of eighteen and SSI-disabled adults as the recipients of federally administered payments who are between the ages of eighteen and sixty-four.

SSI program costs are borne by both the federal government and state governments. Federal costs include federal benefit payments, administrative costs, and costs of beneficiary services. Payment data by age group are available from the 2009 Annual Report of the SSI Program (table IV.C2). Administrative costs, also obtained from the 2009 Annual Report of the SSI Program (table IV.E1), are allocated to SSI-disabled adults and

SSI-disabled children according to their caseload shares. The costs of beneficiary services, such as Vocational Rehabilitation and the Ticket to Work Program, are all allocated to SSI-disabled adults. State costs include state supplementation payments that may be administered federally or by the state. Data on federally administered state payments are obtained from the 2009 Annual Report of the SSI Program (table IV.C4).

AFDC/TANF caseload data are obtained from various Annual Statistical Supplements of the Social Security Administration (SSA, various years a) and the U.S. Department of Health and Human Services for the years since 1996.

The unit used for the AFDC/TANF caseloads-to-population ratio is the percentage of families benefiting from the program; for the disability programs, individual caseloads are divided by the age-appropriate population (under eighteen for SSI-disabled children, eighteen to sixty-four for SSI-disabled adults and SSDI). The per-capita cost measure for all programs is total program costs divided by total U.S. population, in 2008 dollars.

Dutch Program Data

Dutch disability caseload data for employees and the self-employed come from Centraal Planbureau (CPB). Data on the disability program for hand-icapped youth (Wajong) come from Uitvoering Werknemersverzekeringen [National Social Insurance Institute] (UWV).

Data on Dutch social assistance and unemployment insurance case-loads are also obtained from CPB. The social assistance program (WWB) in the Netherlands is analogous to AFDC/TANF in the United States, in that it is a means-tested social assistance program administered by municipalities. Since 2004, it has been paid for by block grants to munic-ipalities. The unemployment insurance program (WW) in the Nether-lands is administered by the UWV and provides wage-related benefits to insured employees for three to thirty-eight months, depending on work history.

Caseload-to-Worker Ratio

To calculate the number of beneficiaries per thousand workers, we use the economically active population, as defined by the International Labour Organization, as the denominator for both the U.S. and Dutch series. The economically active population comprises "all persons of either sex who furnish the supply of labor for the production of goods and services during a specified time-reference period."

The total number of disability beneficiaries in the United States ages fifteen to sixty-four is the sum of SSDI recipients ages fifteen to sixty-four, SSI-disabled adults ages eighteen to sixty-four, and SSI-disabled children ages fifteen to eighteen.

The total number of disability beneficiaries in the Netherlands ages fifteen to sixty-four is the sum of beneficiaries under employee insurance for long-term disability (WAO/WIA), beneficiaries under the Self-Employed Persons Disability Benefits Act (WAZ), and beneficiaries of assistance for handicapped young persons (Wajong). The combination of beneficiaries under WAO/WIA and WAZ make up the disability-based social insurance caseloads, while Wajong beneficiaries make up the disability-based welfare caseloads.

Total cash-transfer program caseloads in the Netherlands are the sum of caseloads of disability-based programs (WAO/WIA/WAZ/Wajong), the means-tested social assistance program, and unemployment insurance.

Notes

Introduction

1. The 2010 Social Security Trustees Report on the Status of the Social Security and Medicare Programs reports that the SSDI Trust Fund is projected to become exhausted in 2018, two years earlier than the 2009 report projected. Noting the SSDI's deteriorating financial condition, the Social Security Trustees conclude, "Changes to improve the financial status of the DI program are needed soon" (Social Security and Medicare Boards of Trustees 2010). The Congressional Budget Office report confirmed this view (CBO 2010b).

2. Any book arguing for systemic changes in a major government policy will be controversial, but one arguing for such changes in policies toward people with disabilities will be even more so. This is because of the strong social commitment in the United States to mitigating the negative effects of health-based impairments on this population's employment and income. It is also because the data necessary to determine fundamental facts, such as the size of the working-age population with disability, its employment rate, its program participation rate, and the income of the households in which this population lives, are not easily obtainable and are the subject of substantial dispute. For instance, in 2008, after a decade of study, the Bureau of Labor Statistics introduced a new six-question sequence into the monthly Current Population Survey's Basic Monthly Survey (BMS) for the purpose of determining the working-age population with disabilities. (For an example of findings using these data, see U.S. Bureau of Labor Statistics 2011.) This set of questions does not include the traditional work-limitation question the March CPS Annual Social and Economic Survey (ASEC) has used since 1981 and that we use to obtain the statistics reported in this book. Using data from both the BMS and ASEC components of the 2010 CPS, Burkhauser, Houtenville, and Tennant (2011) show that levels of employment and income of the disability population based on the new six-question sequence are substantially higher, while their SSDI and SSI program participation rates are substantially lower, than the outcomes found when using the work-limitation question to determine this population. This is the case largely because these six

124

questions capture only 63 percent of the CPS population that reports receiving SSDI or SSI benefits. Once the work-limitation question is added, the disability population based on the seven questions captures 92 percent of the SSDI-SSI population in the CPS. For a discussion of the controversy surrounding the use of CPS data to capture the working-age population with disabilities, see Hale (2001), Burkhauser, Daly, Houtenville and Nagris (2002), and Burkhauser, Houtenville, and Tennant (2011).

3. Between 1970 and 2010, the number of SSDI beneficiaries more than tripled, from 2.7 million to 9.7 million, far outpacing growth in the working-age population. Between 1974 and 2010, the number of SSI-disabled adults beneficiaries rose from 1.5 million to 4.3 million and the number of SSI-disabled children beneficiaries rose from 71,000 to 1.2 million (Social Security Administration, various years a).

4. SSDI and SSI beneficiaries are allowed to work in small amounts and even encouraged to do so once they have been admitted into the program. However, the data suggest that most do not work, in part because it is difficult to reenter the workforce after a prolonged absence related to qualifying for benefits.

Chapter 1: The Economic Status of People with Disabilities

1. Not everyone with a disability qualifies for disability benefits. As we show in chapter 3, the relationship between the prevalence of disability and the number of applications and acceptances for disability benefits is not straightforward and can be influenced by a variety of factors.

2. The phrase "substantial gainful activity" has a very precise meaning that we describe in chapter 3.

3. The changes in welfare leading up to reform in 1996 began in the early 1990s and were carried out under special waivers granted for states to test work-focused demonstration projects.

4. The U.S. Supreme Court decided *Sullivan v. Zebley*, 493 U.S. 521, on February 20, 1990. The case involved the determination of childhood Social Security disability benefits. In the decision, the Supreme Court ruled that substantial parts of the SSI program's regulation determining disability for children were inconsistent with the Social Security Act, particularly, the statutory standard of "comparable severity."

5. For a more detailed analysis of caseload growth in SSDI, see Bound and Burkhauser (1999); for a more detailed analysis of SSI caseload growth, see Daly and Burkhauser (2003). For a detailed discussion of the political process leading to welfare reform, including changes in the SSI-disabled children program, see Haskins (2006b).

6. AFDC caseloads began to drop in late 1993 and 1994 as states began to obtain waivers from the federal government that allowed them to spend AFDC funds on prowork programs.

7. For complete details on how we capture the working-age population with and without disabilities, see the Data Appendix.

8. Since incomes often lag changes in gross domestic product (GDP), the troughs in median household size–adjusted income we compare here do not correspond exactly to the NBER recession dating. While the NBER has declared that the 2007 recession ended in 2009, history suggests that median income data could continue to decline.

9. Employment is defined as having worked at least 200 hours in the previous year. We used this relatively low cutoff point for defining employment to capture even minor amounts of work effort. Using a stricter definition does not alter the pattern of increase for single mothers, but it does increase the rate of decline in employment for those with disabilities.

Chapter 2: Lessons from Welfare Reform

1. There were also concerns that AFDC was inducing out-of-wedlock births. See Haskins (2006a) for a detailed account of the politics surrounding AFDC policy and the legislative history of the creation of TANF.

2. During the mid-1980s, there were also attempts to induce single mothers to work by unlinking AFDC benefits from health insurance benefits.

3. See Meyer and Rosenbaum (2000) for a more thorough treatment of the relative returns to work versus benefit receipt following welfare reform. In general, they show that expansions in the EITC increased monetary incentives for single mothers to work beginning in the late 1980s and increasing after the 1996 reforms.

4. For a complete discussion of the effects of welfare reform see Blank (2002, 2007) and Moffitt (2003, 2008).

5. Another possibility is that eligible individuals are deterred from applying because of stigma related to receiving welfare benefits or due to a desire to save the limited lifetime benefits in case of more severe future hardship. See GAO (2010a) for a more detailed examination of these issues.

Chapter 3: The Adult Disability Determination Process and Growing Adult Disability Rolls

1. In earlier chapters we defined the working-age population as ages twenty-five to fifty-nine, a common definition in the United States. Here we define the active working-age population as ages fifteen to sixty-four, the definition of working age used by the Organisation for Economic Co-operation and Development (OECD). We do this to enable consistent comparisons with the Netherlands in chapter 5.

2. One other general factor also influences trends in disability program growth: changes in business-cycle conditions. While, in principle, disability

eligibility rules and their interpretation should not be influenced by economic conditions, application and acceptance rates for SSDI generally rise with the unemployment rate. We will discuss this relationship only in passing in this book, however.

3. Table 3-1 uses a representative subsample of NHIS working-age respondents for the years 1983–96 based on their responses to a set of questions about specific impairments. Because the NHIS stopped asking for such detailed information about impairments after 1996, it is not possible to update this information.

4. While the list of physical limitations is fairly comprehensive, the list of mental limitations is much less so and includes mental retardation but not mental illness.

5. Some policymakers would make the case that these insights have influenced policy and led to programs such as Ticket to Work and other work-based programs targeted at SSDI and SSI beneficiaries. As we argue in chapter 4, these types of policy responses, which provide work assistance only after a person has taken months or even years to complete the process necessary to be certified as unable to perform any substantial gainful activity, are likely to be too late to influence work behavior on a large scale.

6. Interested readers can consult several sources of information in the economics literature documenting the influence of both economic conditions and policy changes on disability program growth in the United States. See Burkhauser and Haveman (1982); Stapleton and others (1998); Bound and Burkhauser (1999); Black, Daniel, and Sanders (2002); Brown (2002); Autor and Duggan (2003); Stapleton and Burkhauser (2003a); and Duggan and Imberman (2008). For a nontechnical summary of these issues, see CBO (2010a). For an earlier discussion of how changes in disability policy affect workers' benefit receipt and labor-force participation in OECD countries, see Haveman, Halberstadt, and Burkhauser (1984); Aarts, Burkhauser, and de Jong (1996); and Mulligan and Wise (2011).

7. Congress changed the SSDI-benefit calculation so the net replacement rate for a disabled worker with median earnings increased from 35 percent at the start of the 1970s to 49 percent at the end. Autor and Duggan (2003) argue that increases in the average SSDI/SSI benefit relative to the wages of less-skilled workers are also responsible for the rise in beneficiaries in later years.

8. Although often attributed to the Reagan administration, these changes were enacted under the Carter administration and carried out during Reagan's first term. See Berkowitz and Burkhauser (1996) for a more thorough discussion of this period.

9. Even if evaluating mental illness were clear-cut, relaxing the medical-listing standards for mental illness would have increased the potentially eligible SSDI/SSI population. Because mental illness is much more difficult to evaluate than other conditions with respect to ability to work, this change also increased the number of marginal cases that had to be evaluated and the outcomes of

which could be affected by other factors. Musculoskeletal conditions form another category that is difficult to evaluate with respect to ability to work. For a discussion of the inherent difficulty in establishing medical listings and of changing them over time as best practices change, see the Institute of Medicine (IOM 2007).

10. For a discussion of the political process that led to the changes in the SSI-disabled children program see Haskins (2006b).

11. The SSA is continually revising these standards. Typically, this is done by enlisting the IOM to form a scientific panel to recommend changes. For examples of such recommendations and the evidence supporting them, see IOM (2002 and 2007).

12. These two disability groups have proven to be the most problematic for administrators attempting to establish a clear relationship between severity and inability to work. For a more thorough discussion, see IOM (2007).

13. See Berkowitz and Burkhauser (1996) for a discussion of disability policy over this period.

14. Duggan and Imberman (2008) reach a similar conclusion using a shift-share model to determine the relative effects of changes in age structure, economic conditions, relative generosity of program benefits, and policy changes on SSDI program growth. They find that while all of these factors increased program growth between 1984 and 2004, the most important factor by far in explaining SSDI growth over this period are the programmatic changes discussed in this chapter. They find that liberalization of SSDI eligibility criteria can explain 38 percent of the growth in SSDI receipt among women and 53 percent of SSDI program growth among men.

Chapter 4: Disability Policy and Disability Decision Making

1. In 2009, SSDI benefit payments exceeded SSDI payroll tax receipts and interest from the trust fund beginning the expected drawdown of the SSDI trust fund. The 2010 Social Security Trustees Report projects that the SSDI trust fund will be exhausted in 2018 (Social Security and Medicare Boards of Trustees 2010).

2. Several factors affect future earnings. Future wage earnings are greater for younger workers with more years of work ahead of them, for workers with higher current wage rates, and for workers less likely to be unemployed in the future. Workers who are not employed at the time of a health shock are generally less likely to try to return to work since their future wage earnings, other things equal, are lower than those of workers who are employed at the time of their health shock. See Burkhauser, Butler, and Weathers (2002) for a more formal model outlining the factors in a worker's decision to apply for Social Security benefits.

3. While SSDI benefits are initially set via the SSA's average indexed monthly earnings (AIME) formula to account for real growth in wage earnings over time, once benefits are taken, a worker's primary insurance amount (PIA) increases only to account for inflation. This means that delaying the claiming decision results in higher benefit levels. For younger workers especially, claiming early in life sets them at a benefit level that will stay constant in real terms but fall relative to their age cohort as long as the economy generates real wage growth. In these circumstances, the cost of taking benefits is larger than the simple single-period difference in benefits and potential wage earnings. See Armour, Burkhauser, Daly, and Kwok (2010) for a discussion of the potential benefits of work for children aging out of the SSI-disabled children program.

4. For a review of this literature, see Bound and Burkhauser (1999), Stapleton and Burkhauser (2003b), and Autor and Duggan (2003, 2006). Burkhauser, Butler, and Gumus (2004) provide a full structural model of the decision to apply for SSDI following the onset of a disability that takes into consideration how accommodation affects this decision.

5. Burkhauser, Schmeiser, and Weathers (forthcoming) find that, contrary to popular perceptions, most accommodations do not involve changing physical barriers. Rather they are primarily related to a change in the requirements of the job. Of the 30 percent of workers who were accommodated by their employer after experiencing the onset of a work limitation in the years after the implementation of the ADA in 1992, they found that the vast majority of accommodations were getting someone to help with the job, allowing more breaks and rest periods, allowing a change in coming to and leaving work, allowing a change in the job to something the worker could do, or allowing for a shorter workday. While these accommodations were not costly for the firm in the sense of explicit expenditures, for the majority of firms that did not provide such accommodations, the accommodations may have been too costly with respect to the workplace routine.

6. For instance, Burkhauser, Schmeiser, and Weathers (forthcoming) find that workers whose work limitations were caused by an accident on the job and who are, hence, more likely to be covered by WC are more likely to be offered accommodation by their employer.

7. Berkowitz and Burton (1970) and Burton and Berkowitz (1971) provide the first modern discussion of the economic efficiency arguments for a government mandated WC program funded by experience rating of firms based on their employees' use of program benefits. In those papers, they stress that experience rating leads to the optimal expenditures on safety and accident prevention and health procedures, to the allocation of costs of disability to the source of the injury and into the price of the product, and to the optimal incentives for the maximum labor-force participation of disabled workers. For a more recent discussion of the importance of experience rating on firms' investment in safety

and to engage in claims management, see Thomason (2005); Burton (2009); and Ruser and Butler (2010). We will return to these issues in chapter 7.

8. Berkowitz and Burton (1970) and Burton and Berkowitz (1971) were the first to consider efficiency arguments for experience rating SSDI. They argued that in the case where movement onto the SSDI rolls was based on an incident that occurred at the current firm's workplace and all other causes for movement into SSDI by current workers at a firm are random across all workers, using experience rating would be efficient. The actual experience rate would effectively amount to a flat-rate tax on all firms to finance SSDI benefits for off-the-job events and an experience-rated tax on each firm to finance work-related injuries. While the U.S. SSDI program is not experience rated, a number of European Union countries use some form of premium variation based on experience rating to fund their disability insurance systems. For a detailed discussion, see European Agency for Safety and Health at Work (2010). In chapter 7, we will return to the merits of experience rating for SSDI and will discuss the likely behavioral effects it would have on firm hiring if employers could systematically discriminate (statistical discrimination) against new hires based on the likelihood that they would move onto the SSDI rolls in the future not related to a workplace incident.

9. About 33 percent of workers had access to long-term disability coverage in 2009 (BLS 2009).

10. Burkhauser and Daly (2002) and Daly and Bound (1996) found that only a minority of employers provided accommodations to their workers before the passage of the ADA. Burkhauser, Schmeiser, and Weathers (forthcoming) found that this was also the case before the passage of state disability antidiscrimination laws and state-level accommodation laws, and that these and the ADA increased the likelihood that a worker would be accommodated following the onset of a disability. Nonetheless, a large percentage of those who experience the onset of a disability are not accommodated by their employers. For a more thorough discussion of the literature on how the ADA affected the employment of working-age people with disabilities, see Stapleton and Burkhauser (2003b).

11. Because SSI is a means-tested program, it provides a guarantee of $674 dollars per month. But a dollar of SSI benefits is deducted for every dollar of SSDI benefits received after a $20 disregard. Only a small percentage of SSDI recipients also receive SSI benefits.

12. The enactment of the Affordable Care Act of 2010 may change this for some workers. When this act is fully implemented in 2014, stand-alone Medicaid will be available to all persons with income below 133 percent of the poverty line ($29,000 for a family of four in 2009). In addition, highly subsidized health insurance will be available for persons with income below 400 percent of the poverty line via government-regulated private health exchanges.

13. This is a recognized issue that has been confirmed by research; see Schmidt and Sevak (2004) and Wiseman (2010).

14. See Daly and Burkhauser (2003) for a detailed discussion of the SSI program and its interaction with TANF; see Wiseman (2010) for a discussion of the prevalence of caseload shifting between SSI and TANF.

15. For a discussion of how SSI and welfare populations and programs overlap, see Bound, Kossoudji, and Ricart-Moes (1998); Brown (2002); Kauff (2008); Pavetti and Kauff (2006); and Schmidt and Danziger (2009).

Chapter 5: Lessons from Dutch Disability Policy Reforms

1. Note that while the before-tax value is 80 percent, the empirical average after-tax rate payment was 87 percent.

2. For a more thorough discussion of this early period of disability policy in the Netherlands, see Aarts and de Jong (1992) and Aarts, Burkhauser, and de Jong (1992).

3. See Aarts, Burkhauser, and de Jong (1996, 1998) and Marin, Prinz, and Queisser (2004) for a more thorough discussion of disability policy in the Netherlands over this period.

4. There was a brief overlap between these programs: WIA began in 2004, but WAO did not disappear until 2006.

5. While all firms are free to buy insurance coverage, only smaller firms do so, at least for sickness benefit coverage; most larger firms tend to self-insure.

6. For a more detailed history of Dutch disability policy since 2002, see de Jong (2008).

7. Autor and Duggan (2010) use the recent Dutch reforms as a model for their proposal to mandate U.S. employers to provide short-term disability insurance for their workers.

8. A recent review documents that ten of the twenty-seven European Union countries use premium variations based on experience rating to fund part of their disability program—Belgium, Bulgaria, Czech Republic, Finland, France, Germany, Italy, Netherlands, Poland, and Portugal. See European Agency for Safety and Health at Work (2010).

Chapter 6: Disability Policy for Children

1. See Daly and Burkhauser (2003) for a discussion of the equity issues that arise from offering cash support to the subset of low-income families with disabled children.

2. Wiseman (2010) argues that this is a shortcoming of the SSI-disabled children program and suggests that making it a service-provision benefit would be an appropriate policy change.

3. This same rationale was expressed in a 1996 review of the SSI-disabled children program by the National Academy of Social Insurance. Describing the

program, the report states: "[The] rationale . . . is to level the playing field between families with disabled children and others by meeting some of the added disability-related costs of care as well as basic necessities; to promote family preservation; to compensate for some of the opportunity costs of forgone earnings to care for a disabled child; and to promote community integration and awareness, with long-term beneficial results for both the child and the community" (Mashaw, Perrin, and Reno 1996, 16).

4. At the time, the Senate Finance Committee opposed including children in the SSI program, arguing that their needs were mostly health-based and could be covered by Medicaid. This view lost against the argument that low-income families with a disabled child were among the most disadvantaged in the United States. See Mashaw, Perrin, and Reno (1996) and Daly and Burkhauser (2003) for a more complete discussion.

5. These measures provide an approximation of take-up rates for SSI that we believe is useful in establishing broad trends. Income eligibility is defined based on the official U.S. Bureau of the Census poverty calculations and shows the share of SSI-disabled children as a fraction of children living in poverty.

6. The Supreme Court decision in the case of *Sullivan v. Zebley* (1990) greatly expanded the disability eligibility criteria for children, resulting in substantial subsequent growth in caseloads. We discuss the influence of this decision later in this chapter. See Daly and Burkhauser (2003) for a detailed treatment of the rolls and eligibility criteria.

7. Although there has been considerable focus on the increased rates of childhood obesity and childhood asthma, the data on trends in health suggest that these ailments or illnesses may be replacing others such that, while there is a change in the composition of impairments, there is no change in the aggregate trend in health.

8. Following the *Zebley* decision, a large number of previously denied cases were reassessed and awarded disability benefits. This is evident in the rapid rise in caseloads presented in figure 6-1.

9. When the new rules were applied in 1997, some previously allowed cases became denials. This can be seen in the dip in caseloads evident in figure 6-1.

10. Recent health insurance reforms will likely affect this reason for applying for benefits. Based on the reforms, individuals below 133 percent of the poverty line will be eligible for Medicaid even if working, meaning that fewer families will be motivated to seek SSI-disabled children benefits to receive health insurance. To some extent, the expansion of the State Children's Health Insurance Program (SCHIP) may also reduce health insurance–based entry, but to our knowledge there is no formal research examining this issue.

Chapter 7: Reforming U.S. Disability Policy

1. Since 1980, Congress has required the SSA to conduct demonstration projects to test the effectiveness of possible program changes that could encourage individuals to return to work and decrease their dependence on SSDI benefits. To conduct these demonstrations, Congress authorized SSA, on a temporary basis, to waive certain SSDI and Medicare program rules. The U.S. Government Accountability Office has published a report finding that the SSA has not made effective use of this authority (GAO 2004). Wittenburg, Rangarajan, and Honeycutt (2008) review the outcomes of the major SSA demonstrations conducted under this act and find modest employment gains but little change in exit from the SSDI or SSI programs.

2. This is a model used in many European countries. See Immervol and Förster (forthcoming).

3. The Benefit Offset National Demonstration will test the work responses of current SSDI beneficiaries to a program change that would reduce their benefits by $1 for every $2 earned above a substantial gainful activity threshold amount from the current system.

4. GAO (2010b) discusses the potential value of using experience rating in a U.S. context. Stapleton (2011) proposes experience rating of SSDI payroll taxes along with a series of other reforms to bend the Social Security cost curve. European Agency for Safety and Health at Work (2010) provides a discussion of how experience rating is used in ten European Union countries.

5. As discussed in chapter 4, Ruser and Butler (2010) provide the most recent evidence of the value of experience rating in increasing firms' investment in safety and use of claims management to reduce claims. Burkhauser, Schmeiser, and Weathers (forthcoming) offer evidence that firms provide greater accommodation to workers injured on the job who are presumably eligible for WC than to workers whose impairment was not job related.

6. This book has focused entirely on the two parts of SSI related to disabled adults and the families of disabled children. The third component of SSI is the SSI-older persons program. Since this target population is no longer of working age, we have not focused our attention on it. Unlike the other two SSI programs, its population and costs are falling. For a discussion of this program, see Daly and Burkhauser (2003). However, we see no reason this program could not also be devolved to the states, since the states also have primary responsibility for their older poor citizens.

7. Because SSI payments are financed via general revenues, this would not impact Social Security payroll taxes but would free up SSA resources to be shifted toward activities more in line with its original mission and skills.

8. This method of expanding the EITC was suggested in Burkhauser, Glenn, and Wittenburg (1997).

9. One concern of placing this program under the jurisdiction of states involves determining who will be responsible for defining eligibility criteria for these programs if the SSA is no longer involved. We contend that eligibility is already being determined by state gatekeepers guided by general principles laid out by the SSA. This process could be kept or it could be improved upon through experimentation among states similar to the experimentation that took place prior to the 1996 welfare reforms.

References

Aarts, Leo J. M., and Philip R. de Jong. 1992. *Economic Aspects of Disability Behavior.* Amsterdam: North-Holland.

Aarts, Leo J. M., Richard V. Burkhauser, and Philip R. de Jong. 1992. The Dutch Disease: Lessons for the United States. *Regulation* 15 (Spring): 75–86.

————, ed. 1996. *Curing the Dutch Disease: An International Perspective on Disability Policy Reform.* Aldershot, Great Britain: Avebury, Ashgate Publishing Ltd.

————. 1998. Convergence: A Comparison of European and United States Disability Policy. In *New Approaches to Disability in the Work Place*, ed. Terry Thomason, John Burton, and Douglas Hyatt, 299–388. Industrial Relations Research Association Research Volume. Ithaca, NY: Cornell University Press.

Acemoglu, Daron, and Joshua Angrist. 2001. Consequences of Employment Protection? The Case of the Americans with Disabilities Act. *Journal of Political Economy* 109 (5): 915–57.

Armour, Philip, Richard V. Burkhauser, Mary C. Daly, and Joyce Kwok. 2010. *Understanding the Incentives to Work for Children with Disabilities as They Age Out of the Supplemental Security Income-Disabled Children Program.* Paper presented at the Southern Economic Association, November.

Atkinson, Anthony B., Lee Rainwater, and Timothy Smeeding. 1995. *Income Distribution in OECD Countries. Evidence from the Luxembourg Income Study.* Social Policy Studies no. 18. Paris: Organisation for Economic Co-operation and Development.

Autor, David H., and Mark G. Duggan. 2003. The Rise in Disability Recipiency and the Decline in Unemployment. *The Quarterly Journal of Economics* 118 (1): 157–205.

————. 2006. The Growth in the Social Security Disability Rolls: A Fiscal Crisis Unfolding. *Journal of Economic Perspectives* 20 (Summer): 71–96.

————. 2010. *Supporting Work: A Proposal for Modernizing the U.S. Disability Insurance System.* (December) The Hamilton Project and Center for American Progress: Washington, DC.

Berkowitz, Edward D., and Richard V. Burkhauser. 1996. A United States Perspective on Disability Programs. In *Curing the Dutch Disease: An International Perspective on Disability Policy Reform*, ed. Leo J. M. Aarts, Richard V. Burkhauser, and Philip R. de Jong, 71–92. Aldershot, Great Britain: Avebury, Ashgate Publishing Ltd.

Berkowitz, Monroe, and John F. Burton, Jr. 1970. The Income Maintenance Objectives in Workmen's Compensation. *Industrial and Labor Relations Review* 24 (October): 13–31.

Black, Dan, Kermit Daniel, and Seth Sanders. 2002. The Impact of Economic Conditions on Participation in Disability Programs: Evidence from the Coal Boom and Bust. *American Economic Review* 92:27–50.

Blank, Rebecca M. 2002. Evaluating Welfare Reform in the United States. *Journal of Economic Literature* 40 (4): 1105–66.

———. 2007. What We Know, What We Don't Know, and What We Need to Know about Welfare Reform. National Poverty Center Working Paper Series #07-19.

Blank, Rebecca M., and David Ellwood. 2002. Clinton's Legacy for America's Poor. In *American Economic Policy in the 1990s*, ed. Jeffrey Frankel and Peter Orszag, 749–800. Cambridge, MA: MIT Press.

Blank, Rebecca M., and Brian Kovak. 2008. The Growing Problem of Disconnected Single Mothers. National Poverty Center Working Paper #2007-28 (August).

Bound, John, and Richard V. Burkhauser. 1999. Economic Analysis of Transfer Programs Targeted on People with Disabilities. In *Handbook of Labor Economics*, vol. 3C, ed. Orley C. Ashenfelter and David Card, 3417–3528. Amsterdam: Elsevier Science.

Bound, John, Richard V. Burkhauser, and Austin Nichols. 2003. Tracking the Household Income of SSDI and SSI Applicants. In *Research in Labor Economics*, vol. 22, ed. Sol W. Polachek, 113–59. Stanford, CT: JAI Press.

Bound, John, Sherrie Kossoudji, and Gema Ricart-Moes. 1998. The Ending of General Assistance and SSI Disability Growth in Michigan. In *Growth in Disability Benefits: Explanations and Policy Implications*, ed. Kalman Rupp and David C. Stapleton, 224–48. Kalamazoo, MI: W. E. Upjohn Institute for Employment Research.

Bound, John, and Timothy Waidmann. 2002. Accounting for Recent Declines in Employment Rates among the Working-Aged Disabled. *Journal of Human Resources* 37 (2): 231–50.

Brown, Michael H. 2002. Geographic and Group Variation in Supplemental Security Income. Ph.D. dissertation, University of Kentucky.

Burke, Vee. 1996. New Welfare Law: Comparison of the New Block Grant Program with Aid to Families with Dependent Children. Report No. 96-720EPW. Washington, DC: Congressional Research Service.

Burkhauser, Richard V., J. S. Butler, and Gulcin Gumus. 2004. Dynamic Programming Model Estimates of Social Security Disability Insurance Application Timing. *Journal of Applied Econometrics* 19 (6): 671–85.

Burkhauser, Richard V., J. S. Butler, and Robert R. Weathers II. 2002. How Policy Variables Influence the Timing of Social Security Disability Insurance Applications. *Social Security Bulletin* 64 (1): 52–83.

Burkhauser, Richard V., and Mary C. Daly. 2002. U.S. Disability Policy in a Changing Environment. *Journal of Economic Perspectives* 16 (Winter): 213–24.

Burkhauser, Richard V., Mary C. Daly, and Philip R. de Jong. 2008. Curing the Dutch Disease: Lessons for United States Disability Policy. Working Paper 188, University of Michigan, Michigan Retirement Research Center.

Burkhauser, Richard V., Mary C. Daly, and Andrew J. Houtenville. 2001. How Working-Age People with Disabilities Fared over the 1990s Business Cycle. In *Ensuring Health and Income Security for an Aging Workforce*, ed. Peter P. Budetti, Richard V. Burkhauser, Janice M. Gregory, and H. Allan Hunt, 291–346. Kalamazoo, MI: W. E. Upjohn Institute for Employment Research.

Burkhauser, Richard V., Mary C. Daly, Andrew J. Houtenville, and Nigar Nargis. 2002. Self-Reported Work Limitation Data: What They Can and Cannot Tell Us. *Demography* 39 (August): 541–55.

Burkhauser, Richard V., Shuaizhang Feng, Stephen Jenkins, and Jeff Larrimore. Forthcoming. Recent Trends in Top Income Shares in the USA: Reconciling Estimates from March CPS and IRS Tax Return Data. *Review of Economics and Statistics*.

Burkhauser, Richard V., Andrew J. Glenn, and David C. Wittenburg. 1997. The Disabled Worker Tax Credit. In *Disability: Challenges for Social Insurance, Health Care Financing and Labor Market Policy*, ed. Virginia Reno, Jerry Mashaw, and William Gradison, 47–65. Washington, DC: National Academy of Social Insurance.

Burkhauser, Richard V. and Robert H. Haveman. 1982. *Disability and Work: The Economics of American Policy*. Baltimore: Johns Hopkins University Press.

Burkhauser, Richard V., and Andrew J. Houtenville. 2009. Employment among Working-Age People with Disabilities: What Current Data Can Tell Us. In *Work and Disability: Issues and Strategies for Career Development and Job Placement* (3rd ed.), ed. Edna Mora Szymanski and Randall M. Parker, 49–86. Austin, TX: Pro-Ed, Inc.

Burkhauser, Richard V., Andrew J. Houtenville, and Ludmila Rovba. 2009. Poverty. In *Counting Working-Age People with Disabilities: What Current Data Tell Us and Options for Improvement*, ed. Andrew J. Houtenville, David C. Stapleton, Robert R. Weathers II, and Richard V. Burkhauser, 191–224. Kalamazoo, MI: W. E. Upjohn Institute for Employment Research.

Burkhauser, Richard V., Andrew J. Houtenville, and Jennifer R. Tennant. 2011. Capturing the Elusive Working-Age Population with Disabilities: Who the Six Question Sequence in CPS-BMS and ACS Capture and Who They Miss. Cornell Working Paper (February).

Burkhauser, Richard V., Maximilian Schmeiser, and Robert Weathers II. Forthcoming. The Importance of Anti-Discrimination and Workers' Compensation Laws on the Provision of Workplace Accommodations Following the Onset of a Disability. *Industrial and Labor Relations Review*.

Burkhauser, Richard V., Timothy M. Smeeding, and Joachim Merz. 1996. Relative Inequality and Poverty in Germany and the United States Using Alternative Equivalency Scales. *The Review of Income and Wealth* 42 (December): 381–400.

Burkhauser, Richard V., and David C. Stapleton. 2003. A Review of the Evidence and Its Implications for Policy Change. In *The Decline in Employment of People with Disabilities: A Policy Puzzle*, ed. David C. Stapleton and Richard V. Burkhauser, 369–406. Kalamazoo, MI: W. E. Upjohn Institute for Employment Research.

Burton, John F. Jr. 2009. Workers' Compensation. In *Labor and Employment Law and Economics*, ed. Kenneth G. Dau-Schmidt, Seth D. Harris, and Orly Lobel, 235–74. Cheltenham, UK and Northampton, MA: Edward Elgar.

Burton, John F. Jr., and Monroe Berkowitz. 1971. Objectives Other Than Income Maintenance for Workmen's Compensation. *Journal of Risk and Insurance* 38 (September): 343–55.

Centraal Planbureau [CPB Netherlands Bureau for Economic Policy Analysis]. 1998–2010. http://www.cpb.nl/en/node/.

Congressional Budget Office (CBO). 2007. *Changes in the Economic Resources of Low-Income Households with Children* (May). Washington, DC.

———. 2010a. *Social Security Disability Insurance: Participation Trends and Their Fiscal Implications* (July). Washington, DC.

———. 2010b. *CBO's 2010 Long-Term Projections for Social Security: Additional Information* (October). Washington, DC.

Council of Economic Advisors (CEA). 1997. *Technical Report: Explaining the Decline in Welfare Receipt, 1993–1996*. Washington, DC: Executive Office of the President.

Daly, Mary C. 1998. Characteristics of SSI and DI Recipients in the Years Prior to Receiving Benefits: Evidence from the PSID. In *Growth in Disability Benefits: Explanations and Policy Implications*, ed. Kalman Rupp and David C. Stapleton, 177–196. Kalamazoo, MI: W. E. Upjohn Institute for Employment Research.

Daly, Mary C., and John Bound. 1996. Worker Adaptation and Employer Accommodation Following the Onset of a Work-Limiting Health Impairment. *Journal of Gerontology* 51b (2): s53–s60.

Daly, Mary C., and Richard V. Burkhauser. 2003. The Supplemental Security Income Program. In *Means Tested Transfer Programs in the United States*, ed. Robert Moffitt, 79–140. Chicago: University of Chicago Press and National Bureau of Economic Research.

Daub, Hal. 2002. Statement to the House Committee on Ways and Means, Subcommittee on Social Security. *Reforming the Disability Insurance and Supplemental Security Income Disability Programs*. 107th Cong., 2nd sess. (June 11).

De Jong, Philip R. 2008. Recent Changes in Dutch Disability Policy. APE Working Paper (September).

DeLeire, Thomas. 2000. The Wage and Employment Effects of the Americans with Disabilities Act. *Journal of Human Resources* 35 (4): 693–715.

Donohue, John J. III, and James J. Heckman. 1991. Continuous versus Episodic Change: The Impact of Civil Rights Policy on the Economic Status of Blacks. *Journal of Economic Literature, American Economic Association* 29 (December): 1603–43.

Duggan, Mark, and Scott Imberman. 2008. Why Are the Disability Rolls Skyrocketing? The Contribution of Population Characteristics, Economic Conditions, and Program Generosity. In *Health at Older Ages: The Causes and Consequences of Declining Disability among the Elderly*, ed. David Cutler and David Wise, 337–80. Chicago: University of Chicago Press.

Ellwood, David T. 2003. Working with Welfare: The Transformation of U.S. Social Policies. In *Small Transformations: The Politics of Welfare Reform—East and West*, ed. Janos Matyas Kovacs, 244–60. Münster: Lit Verlag.

European Agency for Safety and Health at Work. 2010. *Economic Incentives to Improve Occupational Safety and Health: A Review from the European Perspective*. Luxembourg: Publication Offices of the European Union.

Everhardt, Tom, and Philip R. de Jong. Forthcoming. Return to Work after Long Term Sickness: The Role of Employer Based Interventions. *De Economist [Netherlands Economic Review]*.

Garrett, Alma. B., and Sherry H. Glied. 2000. Does State AFDC Generosity Affect Child SSI Participation? *Journal of Policy Analysis and Management* 19 (2): 275–95.

Goodman, Nanette, and Timothy Waidmann. 2003. Social Security Disability Insurance and the Recent Decline in the Employment Rate of People with Disabilities. In *The Decline in Employment of People with Disabilities—A Policy Puzzle*, ed. David C. Stapleton and Richard V. Burkhauser, 339–68. Kalamazoo, MI: W. E. Upjohn Institute for Employment Research.

Government Accountability Office (GAO). 1994. *Rapid Rise in Children on SSI Disability Rolls Follows New Regulations*. Washington, DC.

———. 1995. *New Functional Assessments for Children Raise Eligibility Questions*. Washington, DC.

———. 1997. *SSA Must Hold Itself Accountable for Continued Improvement in Decision-Making*. Washington, DC.

———. 1998. *Welfare Reform: States Are Restructuring Programs to Reduce Welfare Dependence*. Washington, DC.

———. 2001. *Welfare Reform: Progress in Meeting Work-Focused TANF Goals*. Washington, DC.

———. 2004. *Improved Processes for Planning and Conducting Demonstrations May Help SSA More Effectively Use Its Demonstration Authority*. Washington, DC.

———. 2010a. *Implications of Caseload and Program Changes for Families and Program Monitoring*. Washington, DC.

———. 2010b. *Highlights of a Forum: Actions That Could Increase Work Participation for Adults with Disabilities*. Washington DC (GAO-10-812SP) (July).

Hale, Thomas W. 2001. The Lack of a Disability Measure in Today's Current Population Survey. *Monthly Labor Review* 124 (6): 38–40.

Haskins, Ron. 2006a. Congressional Testimony for the House Committee on Ways and Means: The Outcomes of 1996 Welfare Reform. 109th Cong., 2nd session (July 19).

————. 2006b. *Work over Welfare: The Inside Story of the 1996 Welfare Reform Law.* Washington, DC: Brookings Institution.

Haveman, Robert H., Victor Halberstadt, and Richard V. Burkhauser. 1984. *Public Policy toward Disabled Workers: A Cross-National Analysis of Economic Impacts.* Ithaca, New York: Cornell University Press.

Hemmeter, Jeffrey, Jacqueline Kauff, and David C. Wittenburg. 2009. Changing Circumstances: Experiences of Child SSI Recipients before and after Their Age-18 Redetermination for Adult Benefits. *Journal of Vocation Rehabilitation* 30 (3): 201–21.

Hotchkiss, Julie L. 2003. *The Labor Market Experience of Workers with Disabilities: The ADA and Beyond.* Kalamazoo, MI: W. E. Upjohn Institute of Employment Research.

————. 2004. A Closer Look at the Employment Impact of the Americans with Disabilities Act. *Journal of Human Resources* 39 (4): 887–911.

Houtenville, Andrew J., and Richard V. Burkhauser. 2005a. Did the Employment of Those with Disabilities Fall in the 1990s and Was the ADA Responsible? APPAM Meeting, Washington, DC (November).

————. 2005b. Did the Employment of Those with Disabilities Fall in the 1990s and Was the ADA Responsible? A Replication of Acemoglu and Angrist (2001)—Research Brief. Ithaca, NY: Cornell University, Research and Rehabilitation Training Center for Economic Research on Employment Policy for Persons with Disabilities.

Houtenville, Andrew J., Elizabeth Potamites, William A. Erickson, and S. Antonio Ruiz-Quintanilla. 2009. Disability Prevalence and Demographics. In *Counting Working-Age People with Disabilities: What Current Data Tell Us and Options for Improvement,* ed. Andrew J. Houtenville, David C. Stapleton, Robert R. Weathers II, and Richard V. Burkhauser, 69–100. Kalamazoo, MI: W. E. Upjohn Institute for Employment Research.

Immervol, Herwig, and Michael Förster. Forthcoming. Minimum-Income Benefits in OECD Countries. In *Counting the Poor: New Thinking About European Poverty Measures and Lessons for the U.S.,* ed. Douglas Besharov and Kenneth Couch. Oxford: Oxford University Press.

Institute of Medicine (IOM). 2002. *Visual Impairments: Determining Eligibility for Social Security Benefits.* Washington, DC: National Academies Press.

————. 2007. *Improving the Social Security Disability Decision Process.* Washington, DC: National Academies Press.

International Labour Organization. 1998–2010. LABORSTA Labour Statistics Database.

Jolls, Christine, and J. J. Prescott. 2005. Disaggregating Employment Protection: The Case of Disability Discrimination. Harvard Public Law Working Paper No. 106 (February).

Kauff, Jacqueline. 2008. Assisting TANF Recipients Living with Disabilities to Obtain and Maintain Employment. Mathematica Policy Research, final report. MPR Reference Number 6303-005.

Kubik, Jeffrey D. 1999. Incentives for the Identification and Treatment of Children with Disabilities: The Supplemental Security Income Program. *Journal of Public Economics* 73: 187–215.

London, Rebecca. 1998. Trends in Single Mothers' Living Arrangements from 1970 to 1995: Correcting the Current Population Survey. *Demography* 35 (1): 125–31.

Loprest, Pamela, and David Wittenburg. 2007. Post-Transition Experiences of Former Child SSI Recipients. *Social Service Review* 81 (4): 583–608.

Marin, Bernd, Christopher Prinz, and Monika Queisser, ed. 2004. *Transforming Disability Welfare Policies: Toward Work and Equal Opportunity*. Burlington, VT: Ashgate Publishing Co.

Mashaw, Jerry L., James M. Perrin, and Virginia P. Reno, ed. 1996. *Restructuring the SSI Disability Program for Children and Adolescents*. Washington, DC: National Academy of Social Insurance.

MDRC. 2008. The Social Security Administration's Youth Transition Demonstration Projects: Profiles of the Random Assignment Projects. Contract No. SS00-05-60084.

Meyer, Bruce D. 2010. The Effects of the EITC and Recent Reforms. In *Tax Policy and the Economy* vol. 24, ed. Jeffrey Brown, 153–80. Cambridge, MA: MIT Press.

Meyer, Bruce D., and Dan T. Rosenbaum. 2000. Making Single Mothers Work: Recent Tax and Welfare Policy and Its Effects. *National Tax Journal* 53: 1027–62.

Meyer, Bruce D., and James X. Sullivan. 2008. Changes in the Consumption, Income, and Well-Being of Single Mother Headed Families. *American Economic Review* 98 (5): 2221–41.

Moffitt, Robert A. 2003. The Temporary Assistance for Needy Families Program. In *Means-Tested Transfer Programs in the United States*, ed. Robert Moffitt, 291–363. Chicago: University of Chicago Press and National Bureau of Economic Research.

———. 2008. Welfare Reform: The U.S. Experience. *Swedish Economic Policy Review*, 14 (2): 11–54.

Mulligan, Kevin, and David Wise. 2011. Social Security and Retirement around the World: Mortality and Health, Employment, and Disability Insurance Participation and Reforms. NBER Working Paper 16719.

National Center for Health Statistics. 2010. *Health, United States, 2009: With Special Feature on Medical Technology*. Hyattsville, MD: NCHS.

Organisation for Economic Co-operation and Development. 2003. *Transforming Disability into Ability: Policies to Promote Work and Income Security for Disabled People*. Paris: Organisation for Economic Co-operation and Development.

Pavetti, LaDonna A., and Jacqueline Kauff. 2006. When Five Years Is Not Enough: Identifying and Addressing the Needs of Families Nearing the TANF Time Limit in Ramsey County, Minnesota. Mathematica Policy Research, Washington, DC.

Prinz, Christopher, and William Tompson. 2009. Sickness and Disability Benefit Programmes: What is Driving Policy Convergence? International Social Security Review 62 (October/December): 41–61.

Ruggles, Patricia. 1998. A Brief History of the AFDC Program. Washington, DC: Assistant Secretary for Planning and Evaluation, DHHS.

Ruggles, Steven, J. Trent Alexander, Katie Genadek, Ronald Goeken, Matthew B. Schroeder, and Matthew Sobek. 2010. Integrated Public Use Microdata Series: Version 5.0 [Machine-readable database]. Minneapolis: University of Minnesota.

Rupp, Kalman, and Steven Ressler. 2009. Family Caregiving and Employment among Parents of Children with Disabilities on SSI. Journal of Vocational Rehabilitation 30 (3): 153–75.

Ruser, John, and Richard Butler. 2010. The Economics of Occupational Safety and Health. Foundations and Trends in Microeconomics 5 (5): 301–54.

Schmidt, Lucie, and Sheldon Danziger. 2009. The Supplemental Security Income Program and Material Hardship after the 1996 Welfare Reform. Working paper, University of Michigan, Center for Local, State, and Urban Policy.

Schmidt, Lucie, and Purvi Sevak. 2004. AFDC, SSI and Welfare Reform Aggressiveness: Caseload Reductions versus Caseload Shifting. Journal of Human Resources 39 (3): 792–812.

Social Security Administration (SSA). Various years a. Annual Statistical Supplement to the Social Security Bulletin. Available at www.ssa.gov/policy/docs/statcomps/supplement.

———. Various years b. SSI Annual Statistical Report. Washington, DC.

———. 2009a. Annual Report of the Supplemental Security Income Program. Washington, DC.

———. 2009b. Annual Statistical Report on the Social Security Disability Insurance Program. Washington, DC.

———. 2010a. The 2010 Annual Report of the Board of Trustees of the Federal Old Age and Survivors Insurance and Federal Disability Insurance Trust Funds. Washington, DC.

———. 2010b. Disabled Workers: Applications for Disability Benefits and Benefit Awards. Washington, DC (July). Available at www.ssa.gov/OACT/STATS/table6c7.html.

———. n.d. SSA Youth Transition Demonstration Project. Available at www.ssa.gov/disabilityresearch/youth.htm.

Social Security Advisory Board. 2006. A Disability System for the 21st Century. Washington, DC (September): U.S. Government Printing Office.

———. Forthcoming, 2011. Disability Decision Making: Data and Materials. Washington, DC: U.S. Government Printing Office.

Social Security and Medicare Boards of Trustees. 2010. Status of the Social Security and Medicare Programs: A Summary of the 2010 Annual Reports. Washington, DC (August). Available at www.ssa.gov/oact/trsum/index.html.

Stapleton, David C. 2011. Bending the Employment, Income, and Cost Curves for People with Disabilities. Issue Brief, Center for Studying Disability Policy, Mathematica Policy Research (April).

Stapleton, David C., and Richard V. Burkhauser. 2003a. Contrasting the Employment of Single Mothers and People with Disabilities. Employment Research 10 (July): 3–6.

———, ed. 2003b. The Decline in Employment of People with Disabilities: A Policy Puzzle. Kalamazoo, MI: W. E. Upjohn Institute for Employment Research.

Stapleton, David C., Kevin Coleman, Kimberly Dietrich, and Gina Livermore. 1998. Empirical Analysis of DI and SSI Application Growth. In Growth in Disability Benefits: Explanations and Policy Implications, ed. Kalman Rupp and David C. Stapleton, 29–92. Kalamazoo, MI: W. E. Upjohn Institute for Employment Research.

Suijker, F. W. 2007. Verdubbeling van de instroom in de Wajong: oorzaken en beleidsopties [Doubling of inflows into Wajong: Causes and policy options]. CPB Report No. 156.

Thomason, Terry. 2005. Economic Incentives and Workplace Safety. In Workplace Injuries and Diseases: Prevention and Compensation; Essays in honor of Terry Thomason, eds. Karen Roberts, John F. Burton, Jr., and Matthew M. Bodah, 9–36. Kalamazoo, MI: W. E. Upjohn Institute for Employment Research.

Uitvoering Werknemersverzekeringen [National Social Insurance Institute]. n.d. Available at www.uwv.nl/.

U.S. Bureau of Labor Statistics (BLS). 2009. National Compensation Survey: Employee Benefits in the United States (March).

U.S. BLS Division of Labor Force Statistics. 2011. Table A-6. Employment Status of the Civilian Population by Sex, Age, and Disability Status, Not Seasonally Adjusted. Available at www.bls.gov/webapps/legacy/cpsatab6.htm.

U.S. Department of Commerce, Bureau of the Census. Current Population Survey: Annual Social and Economics Supplement 1976–2010. Washington, DC: U.S. Department of Commerce, Bureau of the Census.

———. 2010. Poverty: Historical Poverty Tables—People. Washington, DC (September). Available at www.census.gov/hhes/www/poverty/data/historical/people.html.

U.S. Department of Health and Human Services (DHHS), Administration for Children and Families. n.d. Temporary Assistance for Needy Families Program (TANF) Caseload Data. Available at www.acf.hhs.gov/programs/ofa/datareports/index.htm.

———. 2008. Indicators of Welfare Dependence: Annual Report to Congress. Washington, DC: Office of the Assistant Secretary for Policy and Evaluation.

————. 2009. *Aid to Families with Dependent Children (AFDC) and Temporary Assistance for Needy Families (TANF)*. Available at http://aspe.hhs.gov/HSP/abbrev/afdc-tanf.htm.

Van Sonsbeek, Jan-Maarten. 2010. Estimating the Long-Term Effects of Recent Disability Reforms in the Netherlands. Working Paper. VU University Amsterdam (August).

Weathers, Robert R. II. 2009. The Disability Data Landscape. In *Counting Working-Age People with Disabilities: What Current Data Tell Us and Options for Improvement*, ed. Andrew J. Houtenville, David C. Stapleton, Robert R. Weathers II, and Richard V. Burkhauser, 27–68. Kalamazoo, MI: W. E. Upjohn Institute for Employment Research.

Wiseman, Michael. 2010. *Supplemental Security Income for the Second Decade. Prepared for conference: Reducing Poverty and Economic Distress after ARRA; The Most Promising Approaches*. Washington, DC: Urban Institute.

Wittenburg, David C., Anu Rangarajan, and Todd C. Honeycutt. 2008. The Help System and Employment Policies for Persons with Disabilities in the U.S. *Revue française des Affaires sociales* 4 (4): 111–36.

World Health Organization (WHO). 2001. *International Classification of Disability, Health and Functioning*. Geneva: WHO.

Index

Acemoglu, Daron, 112
Activity limitation
    children, 89, 90, 90*f*, 91, 92*f*, 93
    international definition of, 39
    work-related, 42, 118, 129n5
ADA (Americans with Disabilities Act)
    (1990), 3, 39, 62, 102, 112
Administrative law judge (ALJ), 50,
    52–53*f*
AFDC (Aid to Families with Dependent
    Children), 21–32, 25*f*, 28–29*f*,
    122
    See also Welfare reform
Affordable Care Act (2010), 130n12
AIME (average indexed monthly
    earnings), 63, 129n3
ALJ (administrative law judge), 50,
    52–53*f*
Americans with Disabilities Act
    (1990) (ADA), 3, 39, 62, 102,
    112
Angrist, Joshua, 112
Average indexed monthly earnings
    (AIME), 63, 129n3

Behavioral/mental disorders,
    See Mental conditions
Beneficiaries, disability
    children, changes in description
      of, 86–87, 93–94
    Dutch review of, 74–75, 77–78
    reevaluation of, 44

totals for U.S., 123
Benefit Offset National Demonstration,
    133n3
Benefits, *See* Cash benefits
Berkowitz, Monroe, 111
Blank, Rebecca A., 32
Block grant funding method, 30, 113,
    115
Burkhauser, Richard V., 110, 112
Burton, John F., 111
Business cycle, 44, 119, 126–27n2,
    126n8

Caseload-per-worker ratio, 70, 77–78,
    123
Caseloads
    costs for U.S. programs, 121–22
    data sources for, 121
    Dutch growth curve, 69–70
    program rules as cause of
      increases, 3–4, 44–53
    SSDI increase in, 11–12, 11*f*,
      35–36, 36f, 69–70, 69f, 105,
      125n3
    SSI increase in, 11–12, 11*f*,
      35–36, 36*f*, 44, 69–70, 69*f*,
      125n3
    trends in reported health and
      work disability, 36–39
    welfare reform effects on, 12, 12*f*,
      13, 27, 30
Caseloads-to-population ratio, 122

About the Authors

Richard V. Burkhauser is the Sarah Gibson Blanding Professor of Policy Analysis in the department of policy analysis and management and a professor in the department of economics at Cornell University. He is an adjunct scholar at the American Enterprise Institute. His research focuses on how public policies affect the economic behavior and well-being of vulnerable populations. He has published widely on these topics in journals of demography, economics and gerontology as well as public policy. He is immediate past president of the Association for Public Policy Analysis and Management.

Mary C. Daly is vice president and head of microeconomic research at the Federal Reserve Bank of San Francisco. She is the director of the Center for the Study of Income and Productivity at the bank. Her research focuses on the micro- and macro-economic impact of public policies. She has published widely on these topics in journals of demography, economics, and health. Daly previously served on the Social Security Advisory Board's technical panel and is a fellow in the National Academy of Social Insurance.